The New York Times

CHANGING PERSPECTIVES

Birth Control

I0880568

EDUCATIONAL PUBLISHING
BOOKS

THE NEW YORK TIMES EDITORIAL STAFF

Published in 2020 by New York Times Educational Publishing
in association with The Rosen Publishing Group, Inc.
29 East 21st Street, New York, NY 10010

First Edition

The New York Times
Alex Ward: Editorial Director, Book Development
Phyllis Collazo: Photo Rights/Permissions Editor
Heidi Giovine: Administrative Manager

Rosen Publishing
Megan Kellerman: Managing Editor
Elizabeth Schmermund: Editor
Greg Tucker: Creative Director
Brian Garvey: Art Director

Cataloging-in-Publication Data
Names: New York Times Company.
Title: Birth control / edited by the New York Times editorial staff.
Description: New York : New York Times Educational Publishing, 2020. | Series: Changing perspectives | Includes glossary and index.
Identifiers: ISBN 9781642822212 (library bound) | ISBN 9781642822205 (pbk.) | ISBN 9781642822229 (ebook)
Subjects: LCSH: Birth control—Juvenile literature. | Contraception—Juvenile literature.
Classification: LCC HQ766.8 B573 2020 | DDC 363.9'6—dc23

Manufactured in the United States of America

On the cover: A doctor discusses different contraceptive options with a patient. From daily hormone combination pills to intrauterine devices, there are many birth control options available to suit different lifestyles and needs; Burger/Canopy/Getty Images.

Contents

CHAPTER 3

War and Change

CHAPTER 4

A New Era for Birth Control

CHAPTER 5

New Technologies

Introduction

IN THE UNITED STATES, birth control has had a long and controversial history. While birth control, also known as contraception, has been around since ancient times, it wasn't always very effective in preventing births. In ancient Greece, for example, a plant known as silphium was believed to prevent conception. We can't be sure if the plant was effective as a contraceptive at all today because silphium was so in demand during ancient times that it went extinct in the second century CE.

For many centuries, scientists, doctors and regular women searched for other safe and effective birth control methods. This search took on a new urgency in the late nineteenth century. During this period, industrialization led to large, overcrowded cities and great suffering and poverty amongst people in urban areas of Europe and the United States. Organizations began to encourage providing funding for birth control, to curb what they saw as the overgrowth of the population. In this way, we cannot think about the development of birth control without thinking of eugenics, or the science of controlling the growth of populations.

One of the figures that became incredibly important in the rise of birth control during this period was Margaret Sanger, whose name you will recognize in many of the articles reprinted here. As a nurse and a mother in New York, Sanger frequently saw immigrant mothers who lived in poverty and bore child after child. These women could not afford to take care of so many children from often unwanted pregnancies, and oftentimes their health would also suffer as a result. At the time, the Comstock Law of 1873 prevented any distribution of "obscene" materials. This included any information about

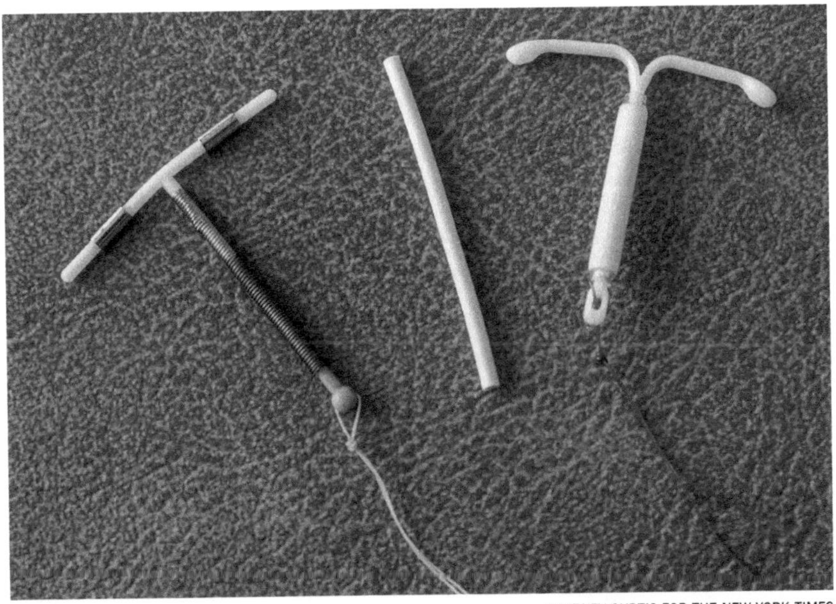

WHITNEY CURTIS FOR THE NEW YORK TIMES

Two types of contraception: intrauterine devices (IUDs), at left and right, and a hormonal implant, center, in September 2014.

family planning and contraceptives. Soon, Sanger set out to overturn this law. In fact, it would be Sanger who would coin the term "birth control" in 1914.

In 1916, Margaret Sanger opened the first family planning and birth control clinic in the United States in Brooklyn, New York, where she introduced women to contraceptive devices such as diaphragms. Sanger was soon arrested, put on trial, and convicted for breaking the Comstock Law by distributing information on birth control. The judge who ruled in the case stated that women do not and should not have "the right to copulate with a feeling of security that there will be no resulting conception." Sanger was put in a working prison for thirty days.

However, change was coming. In 1918, a New York judge ruled that doctors could prescribe birth control to their patients. In 1923, buoyed by this law, Sanger created the first legal birth control clinic in the

United States, which was staffed entirely by female doctors and social workers. Sanger's work eventually morphed into the International Planned Parenthood Federation in 1952, and Sanger was the organization's first president. By this time, researchers were hard at work on making a pill that blocked ovulation in women. In 1951, Sanger met with one of these researchers, Gregory Pincus, and agreed to provide funding for his research. This would lead to the development of the birth control pill, known simply as "the pill." The first contraceptive pill, Enovid, became available in the United States in 1960. This pill would change the course of history.

The pill emerged with a new movement of women's rights and of family planning in the 1960s. Family size in the United States significantly decreased, and women felt that they had more control over their bodies. With decreases in family sizes, women had more opportunities to go back to school and to pursue careers. Taking care of two or three children was quite different from being responsible for eight or ten.

Since its original release in 1960, birth control pills have changed drastically. There are many more available birth control pills on the market now, as well as other contraceptive devices, such as patches, injections and implants. More recently, a birth control pill known as "the morning-after pill" or an emergency birth control pill taken after intercourse, has been approved for use. But this doesn't mean that birth control is no longer a controversial issue. When the U.S. Congress passed the Patient Protection and Affordable Care Act under President Barack Obama in 2010, birth control was mandated to be offered freely by insurance companies. However, some companies refused to provide insurance that would provide birth control to their employees on personal religious grounds. Some prescribers also refused to fill prescriptions for emergency birth control. Many cases have gone to court since 2010 that pit one person's belief that birth control is immoral against the right of women to control their own bodies. The debate still rages on.

CHAPTER 1

The Early Movement

In the early twentieth century, the issue of birth control gained great attention in the United States. This was largely due to the role of pioneering women such as political activists Emma Goldman and Margaret Sanger, the latter of whom would become the most influential American figure in the fight to legalize birth control. For these women, limiting the amount of children women could have was both an issue of women's rights and of economic rights.

Would Limit Families

SPECIAL TO THE NEW YORK TIMES | JUNE 29, 1915

Dr. Hamilton-Muncie says we are becoming a nation of weaklings.

CHICAGO, JUNE 28. — Indiscriminate raising of children is filling the world with the unfit and undermining the stamina of the nation, Dr. Elizabeth Hamilton-Muncie of Brooklyn told members of the American Institute of Homeopathy in annual session today. She declared that families of degenerates were almost twice as large as those of normal persons, and unless remedial legislation were soon forthcoming, Americans would wake up some day to the realization that they were weaklings. Dr. Muncie asserted that physicians should have authority to instruct young people when parentage is proper.

“The law which makes it an offense for a physician to tell parents how to limit the family, though they may be unfit, is as illogical as to say we should not interfere with a falling object because it is acting according to the law of gravity,” Dr. Muncie declared. “This law is a lie. The results of it are seen on every hand in imbecility, insanity, truancy, criminality, arrested mental development, inefficiency, parasitism, and chronic invalidism.

“Persons in these classes are increasing out of all proportion to the normal classes. In normal families the average number of children is four; in degenerate families the average is seven. In New York 25,000 under one year die annually of causes which could be helped by family limitation. But the law says it is better to produce idiots than not to produce at all, and where conditions are the vilest you find breeding the most prolific.”

Talks of Birth Control

BY THE NEW YORK TIMES | APRIL 20, 1916

Rose Pastor Stokes defies law at Emma Goldman dinner.

AT THE EMMA GOLDMAN "Birth Control" dinner at the Hotel Brevoort last night, Rose Pastor Stokes, wife of J. G. Phelps Stokes, declared that because it was a public meeting, she wanted to give out to some woman in the audience information on birth control, as she had been honoring the law by thus breaking it for years. Many diners loudly applauded.

After finishing her talk, Mrs. Stokes went among the auditors and whispered to a number of women, saying afterwards she had given them information about birth control. She also handed out slips of

BETTMANN/GETTY IMAGES

From left to right, Mrs. Rose Pastor Stokes, Mrs. Margaret Sanger and Ethel Byrne, Mrs. Sanger's sister, in court, January 1916. Mrs. Sanger was on trial for mailing her book, "The Woman Rebel," through the mail.

paper on which, she said after the meeting, information about birth control was printed.

Immediately following her announcement to the effect that she had come prepared to give out information on birth control, Mrs. Stokes said:

"I'm not bidding for arrest. I want to do what Emma Goldman did. My being married and now having social standing makes a difference in a way. The press is represented here, but I'm not speaking in a tone of defiance. I want to give out to some woman in this, a public audience, the information that I possess.

"It's really nothing," interposed Mrs. Stokes, amid the deafening cheers of her hearers. "It'll merely break the law and I choose to honor the law by breaking it, and I'm not the only one. There are many other women who'll do that very thing. The courts found it was best to quash the indictments against Margaret Sanger, and it may be that they'll quash the indictment against Emma Goldman. At any rate, we do know that the courts will have a bigger fight than they ever had before."

Birth Control Gets Court Indorsement

BY THE NEW YORK TIMES | OCT. 13, 1916

LEGALIZED BIRTH CONTROL under certain conditions was indorsed yesterday by Judge Wadhams in the Court of General Sessions in suspending sentence upon Mrs. Rebecca Schnur, of 293 Third Street, who pleaded guilty to a charge of burglary. Mrs. Schnur declared that she was compelled to steal to obtain bread for her six children, the youngest of whom was ten months old.

Up until five years ago Samuel Schnur was able to support his family with his earnings as an operator on children's coats in an east side shop. The close confinement ultimately had its effect on the man, and he developed tuberculosis. He kept at his work despite his illness until discovered by an inspector of the Health Department, who refused to permit him to remain in the shop as long as he had the disease. Since that time he has been unable to obtain employment.

The burden of support fell on Mrs. Schnur, who has partially earned a living for the family by doing odd jobs. Recently she was unfortunate in obtaining employment, and quickly used up what little money she had on hand. Last month she entered the home of Morris Moskowitz, at 203 East Seventh Street, and stole a small sum of money and a watch, which resulted in her arrest.

In his opinion Judge Wadhams said that Mrs. Schnur had been found guilty on a previous occasion of theft, arising out of the same conditions, but sentence was suspended. Although the woman could be sentenced for a long term in prison, the Court said that the unusual circumstances were such as to warrant a further extension of clemency.

After discussing the condition of the husband and his inability to care for his family, Judge Wadhams made the following statement:

"Nevertheless he goes on becoming the father of children who have very little chance under the conditions to be anything else but tubercular, and, themselves growing up, to repeat the process with society. There is no law against that.

"But we have not only no birth regulation in such cases, but if information is given with respect to birth regulation people are brought to the bar of justice for it. There is a law they violate."

Judge Wadhams pointed out that many nations of Europe had adopted birth regulation with seemingly excellent results. He queried whether Americans had taken as common sense view of the subject as we might.

"I believe," the opinion continued, "that we are living in an age of ignorance which at some future time will be looked upon aghast as we look back upon conditions which we now permit to exist. So that here we have a family increasing in number, with a tubercular husband, with a woman with a child at her breast, with other small children at her skirts, and no money."

Efforts are being made to provide permanent help for Mrs. Schnur. Temporary help will be given by a charitable society until work can be found for the woman.

Mrs. Sanger Accepts Bail

BY THE NEW YORK TIMES | OCT. 28, 1916

THREE BIRTH CONTROL advocates were released on bail yesterday pending trial on the charge of disseminating information on birth control, and another, Emma Goldman, Anarchist, was held in $500 bail on the same charge, for which she served a term in the Queens County Penitentiary last Spring. Mrs. Margaret Sanger and her assistant, Miss Fannie Mindell, were arrested on Thursday night for spreading birth control information at Mrs. Sanger's birth control clinic, 46 Amboy Street, Brownsville.

Mrs. Ethel Byrne, a widow, and sister of Mrs. Sanger, whose arrest followed that of the others, was arraigned yesterday morning in the New Jersey Avenue Court, Brownsville. She said she was glad to be bailed out. Mrs. Sanger, seen then, said that she would stay in jail until

BETTMANN/GETTY IMAGES

Emma Goldman standing on a car and speaking to a crowd about birth control in Union Square in May earlier this year.

she was brought to trial on Monday. Last night, her counsel gave bail for her and her assistant before Magistrate Voorhis in Brooklyn.

Emma Goldman, accused of circulating literature on birth control at a meeting in Union Square on May 20, was held in $1,000 bail in Yorkville Court by Magistrate Barlow. She said she was a lecturer and lived at 20 East 125th Street. As she had been a witness in a similar case in behalf of her attorney, Bolton Hall, she should not have been arrested, she asserted. Hall was discharged several days ago.

Doctors Divided on Birth Control

BY THE NEW YORK TIMES | NOV. 19, 1916

THE INTIMATION OF John S. Sumner, Anthony Comstock's successor, that the attitude of the Society for the Prevention of Vice on the subject of birth control would be affected to a considerable extent by the stand taken on the subject by the New York County Medical Society aroused much interest yesterday in the question of what action the county society would take at its meeting on Tuesday, Dec. 26, when the question is to come up for discussion.

Officials of the society admitted yesterday that a lively session is in prospect. One important faction is heartily in favor of having the society not only go on record as favoring a plan to allow physicians to give married patients information on the subject of birth control but they want the society to urge that the Penal Law be amended. Another faction is opposed to the whole proposition, while yet another is opposed to physicians making any actual recommendations to the law making bodies regarding the Criminal Code.

Dr. F. E. Sondern, President of the New York County Medical Society, said last night that the subject had come up for discussion in the society last Spring and had been referred to the committee which constitutes the Board of Governors of the organization. This board, he said, reported adversely on it during the early Autumn, but a number of members were not content to let the matter rest there. One introduced a resolution to have Dr. Sondern appoint a committee of nine to present the arguments for both sides in a memorial not to exceed 2,000 words to be read at the December meeting, after which the society was to take action on the subject. The committee was appointed, with Dr. Abraham Jacobi as its Chairman. Dr. Jacobi is one of the best-known physicians of the city and is in favor of the plan to permit the dissemination of the information by licensed physicians.

"The object can be summed up in two lines," Dr. Jacobi said yesterday. "It is to allow every licensed physician to give advice to married people on the question of birth control."

It was pointed out that while this program is not as broad as many of the birth control champions would like, in that it restricts the persons who can give the information to licensed physicians, it would be, in the opinion of its opponents at least, a radical departure for the County Medical Society.

Dr. J. Bentley Squier, Vice President of the society, and said to be slated for election to the Presidency at its meeting on Nov. 27, explained the attitude of the different factions yesterday.

"At present any physician who gives information on this subject is liable to go to jail," he said. "At the same time, however, it must be remembered that if the Penal Code on the subject were altered, it would be possible for unprincipled persons to do a great deal of damage.

"It is my own opinion that such changes in our Penal Code should come from laymen and not from the physicians. If the laymen need this information, it should be their duty to have legislation altered to meet the need and to protect the physician from whom they get it."

Dr. Jacobi's response to Dr. Squier's suggestion that the subject was a matter for laymen was: "I suppose physicians have some rights as citizens, too, haven't they?"

Birth Controllers Up Early for Trial

BY THE NEW YORK TIMES | JAN. 5, 1917

ONE OF THE CASES growing out of Mrs. Margaret Sanger's "birth control" fight reached the courts yesterday when Mrs. Ethel Byrne, sister of Mrs. Sanger, was put on trial in Special Sessions, Brooklyn. The charge against Mrs. Byrne was that she had sold articles the sale of which was prohibited under Section 1,142 of the Penal Law. The sales, it was charged, took place at the "birth control clinic" opened by Mrs. Sanger at 46 Amboy Street, Brownsville, twice raided and closed by the police.

There was a popular supposition yesterday that it was the trial of Mrs. Sanger which was going on before the Brooklyn Court. About fifty women, many of them prominent socially and known as active workers in child welfare work, tendered Mrs. Sanger a breakfast in the Della Robbia room at the Hotel Vanderbilt at 8 o'clock in the morning as a preliminary to her supposed hearing, and a number of them waited in the Brooklyn court room until the trial got under way late in the afternoon. Mrs. Sanger said at the breakfast, according to some of those present, that if convicted she would call herself out on a hunger strike.

Mrs. Amos Pinchot, who is organizing a Committee of One Hundred to aid Mrs. Sanger and to work for legislation making it legal for physicians and nurses to disseminate information on birth control, attended the breakfast. She also waited in Brooklyn until noon for the trial to begin. She said last night that she had understood all the while that it was Mrs. Sanger who was to be tried.

There were three arrests growing out of the raids on Mrs. Sanger's clinic. Mrs. Sanger was held on two charges, one of selling prohibited articles and the other of maintaining a public nuisance, the latter charge growing out of her second arrest, when she reopened the clinic after being released under bail. She appealed for a jury trial and succeeded in having the public nuisance charge sent to the Grand Jury,

BETTMANN/GETTY IMAGES

Mrs. Margaret Sanger in 1916.

where, according to Assistant District Attorney Edward A. Cooper, it will come up next week. Mrs. Byrne was also held on two charges, of selling prohibited articles and of distributing prohibited literature.

Mrs. Byrne's trial got such a late start yesterday that the Justices of Special Sessions adjourned the hearing until next Monday morning. At the conclusion of this case Mrs. Byrne will be tried on the second charge.

Miss Fannie Mindell, a nurse, the third person arrested in connection with the "birth control clinic," will be tried on a charge of distributing prohibited literature at the same time that this charge against Mrs. Byrne is tried. Not until both of these trials have been concluded, according to Mr. Cooper, will Mrs. Sanger be brought before a jury.

The defendants in the trials are being represented by Jonah J. Goldstein of 366 Broadway. He sought a further postponement of the case yesterday morning, but was refused, and about fifteen women of Brownsville, who had been subpoenaed, waited most of the day. All these women seemed to be poor, and some of them carried infants. The trial was not called until 4:10 P.M.

"This is an outrage," exclaimed Miss Helen Todd, one of the social workers who had waited all day for the trial to begin. "Here these poor women have been ordered to come here and told that if they did not come they would be fined $250 and imprisoned for thirty days. They have been unable to care for the infants they have with them, and have had to neglect those at home. Both the mothers and the infants have waited all day with nothing to eat."

The delay caused great indignation among many of the other well dressed women who were waiting for the trial. The women subpoenaed as witnesses had gone to Mrs. Sanger's clinic for information. "They need this information. Heaven knows," said Mrs. Rose Pastor Stokes, one of those who had come as interested spectators. "Most of them have more children now than they can provide for out of their husbands' meagre wages."

One of the women waiting to be called as a witness said she had five children, her husband earned $18 a week, and that she probably would be "beaten up" for getting into anything that kept her away from home all day. Another said she had three children of whom the eldest was three years old, that she had had to leave them home all day and she feared they might play with matches and start a fire, or in some other way injure themselves in her absence. Mrs. Sanger, who was present all day, tried to console the mothers who were there with babies.

At the beginning of the trial Attorney Goldstein offered a motion that the case be dismissed on the ground that the law alleged to have been violated was unconstitutional and arbitrary. He asked for opportunity to present arguments to prove this. Justice Garvin, presiding, said the case was too important to make a decision on this point at once, and decided to permit the argument at the conclusion of the trial.

Assistant District Attorney Cooper presented Mrs. Arthur Whitehouse, a police matron, to testify that at the clinic she bought articles from Mrs. Byrne that were prohibited by the Penal Law. Detectives and policemen were called by the prosecution to testify regarding the arrest and to present circulars and other material that they had seized at Mrs. Sanger's clinic.

The State's aim is to show that the law as it now stands was violated by the defendants.

"It is foolish for them to bring all of these poor women to court to prove that," Mrs. Sanger said while waiting for the trial to begin. "I admit that we disseminated this information, but contend that any law which makes it wrong to aid the poor in this manner is opposed to the constitution of a free people."

Among the women who attended the breakfast and the trial were Miss Alice Carpenter, Mrs. Frank Cothren, Miss Augusta Holland, Miss Elizabeth Stuyvesant, representatives of the National Birth Control League, of the New York Birth Control League, of the Child

Welfare League, of Mrs. Pinchot's new Committee of One Hundred, and of numerous other similar organizations, all of which are planning to co-operate vigorously in the fight for revised legislation on birth control at the coming session of the Legislature.

For State Inquiry Into Birth Control

SPECIAL TO THE NEW YORK TIMES | FEB. 1, 1917

ALBANY. N.Y., JAN. 31. — Governor Whitman will pardon Mrs. Ethel Byrne, the imprisoned birth control advocate, who is on a hunger strike in the penitentiary on Blackwell's Island, if she will promise to refrain from violating the law prohibiting the dissemination of birth control information after her release. The Governor so informed a delegation, headed by Mrs. Amos Pinchot, which appeared before him in the Executive Chamber today to urge that a commission be created to investigate and diffuse accurate information to the public on the subject of birth control.

Mrs. Margaret A. Sanger, sister of Mrs. Byrne and leader of the birth control movement, was a member of the delegation. The Governor said that he thought the community was not anxious to see the suffering of Mrs. Byrne prolonged, especially as, in the absence of an appeal, all her suffering would not help to settle the question of the constitutionality of the law.

"But I am sworn to enforce the law," the Governor added, "and I could grant Mrs. Byrne a pardon only on condition that she would refrain from violating it upon her release."

Mrs. Sanger, who sat with the other women in front of the Governor's desk, shook her head wistfully.

"If the State is willing to take a thousand lives to keep a vicious law on the statute books, I am sure my sister is willing that it should take one more," she said.

After the hearing before the Governor, however, the women in the delegation went to the office of Owen L. Potter, the Governor's legal assistant, and obtained a pardon application and also an order directing Commissioner of Corrections Burdette G. Lewis to permit Mrs. Sanger to visit her sister in prison — a privilege that has been denied her. Mrs. Sanger said she would take the Governor's message to Mrs.

Byrne. Many of the women said that she ought to accept the offer for a pardon.

"She is too precious; we cannot afford to lose her," said Dr. Mary Holton of Gouverneur Hospital. "She can promise the Governor that she will not violate the law in this State, and go over to New Jersey and practice."

The Governor expressed his willingness to appoint the commission the women asked for, after Mrs. Pinchot, Mrs. Sanger, Dr. Holton, and Miss Jessie Ashley had urged the necessity of public education on the subject.

"In the maternity ward of Gouverneur Hospital," said Dr. Holton, "we are compelled to violate the law in order not to commit murder. At that many of our tubercular patients die because, notwithstanding the opinion expressed by Health Commissioner Emerson that this is the proper course to pursue, many of our doctors are unwilling to lay themselves open to arrest even to save the lives of such patients."

Governor Whitman urged that there ought to be an appeal in the case of Mrs. Byrne, and pointed out to the women that this could not be obtained if he granted a pardon.

Mrs. Pinchot filed with the Governor an appeal for amendments to the law to legalize the dissemination of birth control information which had been drafted by Professor John Dewey of Columbia University and signed by thirty-nine Columbia professors and some members of the Faculty of City College. In the delegation besides Mrs. Pinchot, Mrs. Sanger, Dr. Holton, and Miss Ashley were Mrs. Frances Higginson Cabot and Mrs. Maitland Griggs, all members of a Committee of One Hundred formed to conduct an educational propaganda in favor of legalizing the spreading of information regarding birth control.

Birth control caused a flurry in the Assembly this afternoon when Assemblyman Clarence F. Welsh of Albany, his voice quivering with indignation, arose and denounced Mrs. Augusta Cary, Executive Secretary of the National Birth Control League, who has been at the capital for a week sounding members of the lawmaking body on their attitude toward birth control legislation.

"I have here," said Mr. Welsh, waving a pamphlet in his right hand, "an editorial from a magazine on birth control. I understand that there is a woman about the Capitol distributing these pamphlets, which advertise persons who violate the fundamental law of this State and every law of decency and morality. I have learned that she is not registered as a lobbyist. If she does not leave the Capitol I shall call upon the police to arrest her."

Mrs. Cary, who is the mother of two children, hurried from the Assembly Chamber at once. She said afterward that she had been ignorant of the law, but that, after listening to the denunciation by Assemblyman Welsh, she had gone straight to the office of the Secretary of State and entered her name in the list of the lobby.

Mrs. Byrne's physical condition was "good" yesterday afternoon, according to the bulletin which Commissioner Lewis issued after an examination at 4:30 o'clock by Dr. William T. Gibbs. Seventeen and a half ounces of food in all were administered to her, consisting of milk, malted milk, chicken broth, sugar, and a stimulant. Other details of her condition contained in the bullet in were: Blood pressure, 116; temperature, 97.2; heart sound, normal; pulse, 100; respiration, 22.

Commissioner Lewis found a law yesterday under which, he said, Mrs. Byrne might be charged board because of the great expense which her hunger strike has caused.

"If we have people who persist in boarding with us," he said, "I think it would be a wise thing for the city to enforce this provision of law and charge them board, especially if they insist upon lying in bed, instead of working like other prisoners."

Women for Birth Control

BY THE NEW YORK TIMES | OCT. 15, 1920

UTICA. N.Y., OCT. 14. — The climax of today's session of the Woman's Federation and perhaps of the entire week was reached when a resolution was debated and finally passed declaring that "The primary necessity for family, and therefore for public health, is an intelligently determined interval between pregnancies, to be secured by regulating the inception of life and not by interfering with life after it starts," and "urging the speedy removal of all barriers due to legal restrictions, tradition, prejudice or ignorance, which now prevent parents from access to scientific knowledge on this subject, as is possessed by the medical profession."

The debate at times neared disorder, although the President held the convention well in control and prevented more than one speaker at a time. Several votes were taken and each time objections were made as to their legality. The resolution was finally declared carried by a vote of practically three to one.

Want More Babies in Good Families

BY THE NEW YORK TIMES | SEPT. 25, 1921

PRACTICAL MEASURES ADVOCATED by some students to improve races, such as the sterilization of criminals by the X-ray, the promotion of larger families among those of good stock and limitation among others, were discussed at yesterday's session of the International Congress of Eugenics in the American Museum of Natural History.

Major Leonard Darwin, a son of the author of "The Descent of Man," urged the experimental use of the X-ray, with the consent of the subject, to prevent descendants from the feeble-minded and habitual criminals. He suggested segregation for the wastrel, the habitual drunkard and "the work-shy" to prevent the transmission of their traits to future generations.

Major Darwin also urged that the sound and fit and superior people should, by a campaign of patriotism, be induced to raise larger families. Racial deterioration seems evident among all highly civilized peoples, he said, because of the thinning out of the descendants of highly endowed stock and the multiplication of those of inferior endowment.

"The result is anticipated," he said, "that in comparison with the ill-endowed, the naturally well-endowed will, as time goes on, take a smaller and smaller part in the production of the coming generations, with a tendency to progressive racial deterioration as an inevitable consequence. And if we ask whether existing facts confirm or refute this dismal forecast, what do we find? Statistical inquiries, at all events, prove conclusively that, where good incomes are being earned, there the families are on the average small."

History taught, he said, that races in the past had fallen from high estate because of the progressive elimination of their best types.

"I can find no facts," he continued, "which refute the theoretical conclusion that the inborn qualities of civilized communities are deteriorating, and the process will inevitably lead in time to an all-round downward movement."

The only efficient corrective which Major Darwin could think of, he said, was an appeal to patriotism.

UNPATRIOTIC TO LIMIT SOME FAMILIES.

"What is necessary is to make it deeply and widely felt that it is both immoral and unpatriotic for couples sound in mind and body to unduly limit the size of their families," he added.

Major Darwin read this sentence slowly, and at the request of two or three in the audience, read it over again. He said that he believed that such a campaign would succeed, when persons of character and good endowment were awakened to the danger threatening their race.

"The nation that wins in this moral campaign," he said, "will have gone half-way toward gaining a great racial victory."

Major Darwin discussed State policies toward bounties for large families. He said that some good results might be achieved in this way, but that the subject was extremely difficult, because of the danger that premiums on parenthood would increase the families which should be limited and not affect those which should be increased.

Major Darwin argued against the policy of lifting the tax burden entirely from those least able to pay and concentrating it on those better able to pay.

"It follows," he said, "that to increase taxation on the more fit in order to ease the strain of family life among the less fit would do a double dose of harm; that is, by decreasing the output of children where it should be increased and by increasing it where it should be diminished."

Major Darwin said that he would encourage limitation among families in such circumstances that the children did not have a fair chance of healthy growth and education. He said that the problem of dealing with very large families having very small incomes was extremely difficult, but added:

"I can only suggest that State and charitable aid should never be given in profusion as to prevent the appearance of each additional child from causing additional financial strain on the household.

"I hardly know what to suggest, in the case of those who, in spite of this pressure, persist in procreation under evil surroundings, and perhaps for the present we should concentrate attention on the attempt to secure a general approval of the desire to lessen the output of children in such circumstances."

WOULD TAX THE CHILDLESS.

He advocated special taxes on the unmarried and the childless, and said that the feeble-minded in the United States numbered between 300,000 and 400,000. He affirmed that all who had studied the problem agreed that these should be segregated, especially when their natural protectors could not care for them, and be prevented from becoming parents. He called attention to the experiments of the American Stock Breeders' Association in using the X-ray for sterilization.

"It is not for me to discuss what has been done in this respect in the United States, for there are many present who can deal with this subject better than I can," he continued. "We want to know what is the best method of sterilization. Is the X-ray method to be relied on? What effect would it have on the offspring, if insufficiently applied to produce sterility? Is there any danger of cancer as a result? I strongly press this inquiry because I think that the adoption of surgical methods does increase the prejudice against sterilization."

After recommending its experimental use by consent in certain cases, Major Darwin urged segregation by long terms for habitual criminals, to prevent their taking up family life. He said that the statistics of criminologists showed that the child of a criminal was ten times as likely to become a criminal as the child of a normal member of society.

"They have no good qualities to recommend them," he said of habitual criminals, "and the only courage which they show is that needed to face disgrace and imprisonment. Merely to reduce the fertility of this class would be more beneficial than to absolutely prohibit parenthood in the case of a small number of persons convicted of grave crimes."

The elimination of the unfit, the discouragement of large families among the ill-endowed and the encouragement of increased families among the well-endowed, were more practical means of improving race than attempts to breed supermen by efforts to blend superior types, he maintained. If men and women of great natural gifts could be induced to mate, as some eugenists wished, they would be likely to produce a superior generation, possibly including persons of genius, according to Major Darwin, but their excellences in a few generations would become pooled with the common attributes of mankind.

He discussed the classic eugenic experiment of the father of Frederick the Great in recruiting his famous Potsdam Giants by hiring and kidnapping men of huge stature from all over Europe and mating them with large women. This attempt to stock the Prussian army with artificially-bred seven-footers and eight-footers did not make the slightest impression on posterity, so far as known, he said.

BREEDING OF THE TALL FUTILE.

Major Darwin calculated that if the 23,000 tallest men and women in America were mated and induced to rear two children more than the normal family rate, and that if this selection of the tall were continued for centuries, the average height of an American would be increased one inch every 1,500 years. The attempt to raise the average level of intellect and character by breeding experiments, he said, would be equally futile.

"The qualities of selected parents would be due to many factors," he said, "and these factors, like the money of spendthrift descendants of millionaires, would tend to become more and more widely scattered among the people, in accordance with an inevitable law of nature, the final result, we may be certain, being disappointing to the eugenist.

"If we want more persons eminent in morals, intellect or physical strength to spring into existence in all the generations to come, the most certain method of achieving this result would be to raise the level of the whole people in regard to their unborn qualities. For, if this could be done, the factors needed for the reproduction of men of genius would exist in greater numbers; their union by chance in any one individual, or the actual appearance of a man of genius, would occur more often; and all the while lots of people would be receiving the benefits due to their improved natural endowments."

Major Darwin said that undoubtedly persons of high character and intelligence limited their offspring in order to insure them an education and a fair start in life. But he urged such persons to make sacrifices for the good of the race.

"No doubt difficulties will be experienced," he said, "in deciding to what extent the duties of parenthood are imposed in individual cases. The main difficulty, however, will be to get this duty strongly felt by the mass of the people. For success in this endeavor would, I am convinced, have a much greater effect on families than common sense alone would indicate.

"There ought to be a great moral campaign against the selfish regard for personal comfort and social advancement, for these aims must be in a measure sacrificed on the altar of family life, if racial progress is to be insured.

SACRIFICE NEED FOR NATION.

"We must all learn that, if envy and jealousy could be banished, the happiness of our children would depend greatly on their inborn qualities, and but little on their place in society. We should recognize that we should best serve our country by bringing healthy and intelligent children into the world, provided we can give them a sound education and a fair start in life, and all of us should be ready to make some sacrifices of social position in order to obey our country's call in this respect."

Speaking of the general danger of race deterioration in all civilized countries, he continued:

"I cannot refrain from adding that the United States has a mighty future before it, on which the civilization of the whole world may in a large measure depend. It is therefore doubly incumbent on its citizens to consider whether their best or their worst stocks are multiplying most rapidly. If it is the worst stocks, and no steps are taken to remedy it, then this country may in consequence miss an opportunity of filling a most glorious page in the future history of the world."

Dr. Lucien March, Chief Government Statistician of France, pictured the great difficulties faced by France because of her loss of population due to 1,400,000 killed in the war, 800,000 totally disabled, an abnormal death rate among the civil population from 1914 to 1919 totalling an excess of deaths by 400,000, and a reduction of the birth rate below normal during those years totalling 400,000. In 1935, when the thinned out generation born between 1914 and 1919 becomes of working age, France will lack one-sixth of the number of workers which she would have had except for the war.

"In spite of the addition of Alsace-Lorraine," he said, "it is certain that the economic life of the nation will be deprived of an important part of its active forces and will languish for many years if energetic measures are not taken without delay to ward off the threatened deficit in population.

"Without doubt one might temporarily make appeal to foreign workers, but assimilable populations can only furnish a small part.

"Doubtless also the deficit of masculine workers has caused the more general employment of women. But the women who work cannot be fruitful mothers. Feminine work will only be short-lived mitigation."

A number of other eminent speakers addressed the congress, which will resume its sessions in the American Museum of Natural History on Monday.

First Birth Control Clinic to Open Here

BY THE NEW YORK TIMES | NOV. 13, 1921

A BIRTH CONTROL CLINIC, the first in the United States, will be opened in this city next Wednesday, according to an announcement made last night by Mrs. Margaret Sanger at a dinner at the Hotel Plaza in connection with the first American Birth Control Conference, of which Mrs. Sanger is Chairman. The guest of honor was Harold Cox of London, former Member of Parliament and editor of The Edinburgh Review.

The clinic is at 317 East Tenth Street, where four rooms on the ground floor have been leased for a year. A staff of forty physicians has been selected, of whom thirty will be in regular attendance and ten who will act in an advisory capacity. "The little clinic is practically ready to open within the next few days," said Mrs. Sanger.

"The next question will be that of establishing similar clinics in the cities of the various other States of the nation."

After Mrs. Sanger had given a brief outline of the clinic, a collection was taken up, and in a few minutes more than $1,200 was donated. Mrs. Sanger did not give further details in regard to the new clinic, but from Mrs. Anne Kennedy, a member of the committee that arranged the conference, it was learned that the backers of the institution have no fear of the police. "Under a decision of the Court of Appeals," explained Mrs. Kennedy, "Mrs. Sanger was found to have been entirely within the law. The clinic will afford an opportunity to women suffering from a disease, such as tuberculosis, to inform themselves." Mrs. Kennedy further explained that a large staff of doctors was necessary because the plan of those backing the project is to make the clinic immediately a first-class institution for research.

This evening's session of the conference will be held at the Town Hall in West Forty-third Street.

CHAPTER 2

Eugenics and Birth Control

The history of birth control is inseparable from the history of eugenics. As the articles in this chapter illustrate, advocates both for and against birth control used troubling language about controlling the population growth of "less desirable" groups, including the poor and the disabled. Margaret Sanger and other advocates had to appeal to people with such fears in order to get birth control legalized in the United States.

Birth Control's Hunt for Sponsor

BY MARY WARE DENNETT | FEB. 26, 1922

Mary Ware Dennett is the director of the Voluntary Parenthood League.

"WHY DO YOU Americans tolerate that preposterous Comstock Law against birth control?" This is a frequent question asked by observing foreign visitors. They often add that it seems inconsistent with all they have heard about the energy and up-to-dateness of Americans. The amazement increases when it is revealed that Comstock accomplished his now notorious blunder way back in 1873, and that forty-six years elapsed before any definite sustained effort was made to have Congress correct the mistake.

During all these years the United States has had the unfortunate distinction of being the one country in the world which has attempted to keep under legal lock and key the knowledge by which human reproduction may be controlled, and it is the one country whose laws have classed this knowledge with "obscenity."

At intervals there has been protest against the laws, and increasingly all the while the laws have proved to be unenforceable. Shortly after the Federal law was passed a petition with some 40,000 signatures was sent to Congress urging repeal. But as Congress has ever found it easier to err than to acknowledge error, nothing happened.

Individuals and organizations sporadically denounced the laws during a period of about thirty years, while information, despite the law, was more and more circulated among the sophisticated and well-to-do. Then, in 1914, Margaret Sanger made her meteoric appearance. With her vivid demand that the poor who most need instruction as to family limitation should receive it, and with her challenging slogan that a bad law is better broken than kept. Her famous Brownsville clinic for ten days survived its defiance of the law, and then she and her assistant went to jail. In March, 1915, the National Birth Control League was organized. It was committed to the project of securing the needed changes in the laws, both Federal and State, and while the work it did was excellent so far as it went it did not go beyond the preparatory stages of education and agitation, except for two brief sallies to Albany to tackle the New York State law.

In March, 1919, when there was no group anywhere in the country doing legislative work, a new organization was born — the Voluntary Parenthood League. Its first aim was based on the "eventually, why not now" idea, and Item No. 1 on its program was to go straight to Congress and get the Federal law changed; because this change will not only make the circulation of published knowledge possible all over the United States, but it will at one stroke also clear away from twenty-four States the danger that their local obscenity laws, by virtue of the Federal precedent, can be interpreted to prohibit contraceptive information.

In other words, the Federal bill is the key to the situation, the master stroke for the birth control movement, the one act which will wipe out the need for prolonged agitation. In the remaining twenty-four States local legislation will be necessary, but the force of Federal example will make that a relatively simple matter of following suit.

LOOKING FOR A SPONSOR.

Do it, not talk about it, was the galvanizing idea of the league when, three months after organizing, it began the actual canvass of Congress. Leaders and key men in both Houses were interviewed, but chiefly in the Senate, for in that body there was a committee on health, with a physician as Chairman.

The outstanding characteristic of the majority of Congress in their attitude toward this subject proved to be their lack of antagonism. Many have shown embarrassment at first, and many have exhibited every symptom of wishing to side-step responsibility, but it would take less than the fingers of one hand to indicate the number of those who are genuinely opposed. Some of those who began the conversation as noisy enemies have ended either with mild and open minds or as downright friends of the measure, and some needed neither explanation nor argument but promptly acknowledged the measure as sound common sense, and long over-due as well.

The initial interviews served two purposes: one to give the Congressmen a realization that knowledge about the control of parenthood is just the same simple human necessity for all the people as it is for themselves and their own families; the other to enable us to find an advantageous sponsor for the measure.

Most members were quite ignorant as to the exact provisions of the present law and the way Anthony Comstock had originally lobbied the measure through. They didn't know that his proposition had been merely the suppression of pornographic literature and pictures from the sale of which various publishers in the seventies were making large profits, a traffic that was specially directed to college boys.

The samples which Comstock showed to the Congressmen were entirely convincing, and there was wholesale agreement that this sort of smutty stuff should not be allowed in the United States mails.

But Comstock said nothing about what else he had tucked into the bill, namely, the words "preventing conception," and when the bill came up for action in the legislative jam at the end of a crowded session it was passed on sight, few Congressmen knowing that they had thereby prohibited not only the circulation of indecent publications but also the circulation of scientific knowledge on human propagation.

Some members needed to be assured that Congress is not being asked to sanction the interference with life after it has once begun, but merely to free the knowledge as to how the starting of new human life may be controlled. This distinction relieved many Senatorial minds. A fairly frequent worry among the Congressmen has been "race suicide," but they seemed relieved when told such facts as that Holland, with its fifty-two birth control clinics and its established contraceptive instruction which has been going on for more than forty years, had — up to the war — the third highest ratio of increase in population in Europe. A somewhat common type of Senator is he who fears that making contraceptive knowledge legally accessible will result in its abuse, particularly by the young.

But he usually responds quite nobly to such queries as: "If young people are safe only when ignorant, what happens when somehow they get knowledge, as may occur at any moment?" "If American young people, as a whole, are prone to go to the devil as fast as they acquire an understanding of this subject, whose fault is it?" "What is the matter with us elders who have reared them so poorly?" "Isn't knowledge on all subjects capable of abuse, and doesn't safety lie on the far side, not on the near side, of education?"

However, the attitude of the large majority of those interviewed is fairly represented by the letter President Harding wrote when he was a member of the Senate Health Committee, in which he said, "1 have not had time to study carefully the provisions of your bill, but at first reading find myself very much inclined in its favor."

FAMILY LIMITATION.

The one most arresting fact which the Congressmen were asked to face, and which none could deny, was that Congress itself, like any other group of well-to-do men in the United States, already represents the achievement of family limitation despite the laws. The "Who's Who" section of the Congressional Directory does not report Congressmen with families of eight, ten or twelve. Quite otherwise.

A few weeks of quiet but energetic sampling of Senatorial opinions brought us to the point of choosing as the desired sponsor one of the only two physicians of the Senate, a man who had heartily endorsed the bill from the beginning and whose cultured dignity would insure right handling for the measure. But it took him nearly three months to reach the conclusion that he was too occupied with other important issues to do this measure justice. Even then he did not refuse, but merely said he could not yet see his way and urged that some one else be asked. This refusal to refuse has been characteristic of nearly all the fifteen Senators who have been invited in succession to sponsor the bill. All of them believed in it, but in their various ways they have "passed the buck" — some convincingly, some transparently, some gracefully, some awkwardly, but all of them insistent that it was a job better suited to some one else.

Several were "too busy" — among these was one who was not a member of any major committee, who had introduced public-interest bills, and who, as observed from the Senate gallery, sits for hours on end in undisturbed quiet. One assured us he was "too old," another was sure he was "too ignorant of the subject — it needs a man who can give all the data in debate, as I can't." We promised him a perfect arsenal of material, all classified and condensed, but he felt sure he wasn't "equal to doing it well." Another said he was interested, but better not be the sponsor as — "well, candidly, I shall be up for re-election next year, and, you see. ..."

And still another who is considered one of the pillars of the major party in Congress, a physically big man, standing something like six feet three, announced to the relatively small woman who invited him to render this bit of public service, "Really, I'd be afraid to introduce that sort of bill." On being told that he "hardly looked the part," he spent an energetic five minutes trying to blot out the picture of himself as a coward.

A RECEDING PROMISE.

By the time we had secured expressions of approval or favorable inclinations from a majority of the Senate Health Committee, and the promise of the Chairman for a prompt hearing and report, we had achieved a sponsor. He was one of the two physicians in the Senate. This occurred on March 19, 1920. He agreed to introduce the bill "within a week." We urged haste, knowing the plan to adjourn Congress in the early Summer. "Give me just a few days of grace," said he. When many days had passed, so many that grace was conspicuous for its absence, we again said, "Now, please," and again he promised "soon." He steadily reiterated that promise both verbally and in writing, clear up to the end of the session, when Congress adjourned on June 5.

So the sponsor pursuit began anew, and another set of men were discovered who felt themselves "too old," "too ignorant," "too busy" and so forth. But all the while the members were acquiring a better understanding and a more obvious respect for the measure. Almost every one who was consulted responded to our suggestion that, apart from their individual views on the measure, they would do everything possible to insure for the discussion of the question in the cloakrooms, in committee and on the floor an atmosphere of dignity and seriousness which the subject deserved. An influential representative of the old guard Republicans said: "This is a new idea to me as a subject for legislation, and I must give it more thought, but I can see its social importance, and certainly I can assure you right now that I will do my utmost to see that a proper atmosphere for the discussion is established."

More and more men were found whose attitude was like that of a Middle Western leader, who said: "I see no reason why I shouldn't support it." The interviews frequently developed into perfectly good "mothers' meetings." Even the "busy" men often settled down in the big leather chairs of the Marble Room and grew domestically reminiscent. One told how he himself had been "an unwanted baby," a fourth child born when the family lived in one room, and how several of them died, and he became the main support. "And so," he said, "you see there may sometimes be a place for the unwanted ones after all." "Indeed, yes, because brave humans will always struggle to adjust and to triumph, but would you, because of that, deliberately perpetuate the ignorance which keeps on producing unwanted babies?" And he answered unhesitatingly, "No, certainly not."

The men with rural constituents have been specially interested in the need of the country people for good reliable books on the control of parenthood. The mothers and fathers who live miles from a railroad, and who find the only doctor in the nearest village unable or unwilling to give them useful instruction as to how to space their babies, are very real characters to them, and it doesn't take much argument to make them see what our Federal measure will do for these people, and how simple it will make it for them to order by mail, from book stores in the big cities, practical books by the best authorities.

The few instances of hot antagonism became more and more exceptional. Our prize enemy even became friendly enough to suggest easy ways of bringing the measure to vote. But in our first interview he had blurted out remarks such as these, gleaned from our notebook: "You ought to be ashamed, an intelligent American woman like you." "You ought to stay at home and take care of your children" (shades of the suffrage days!). He refused to be diverted from personal abuse by statistics from the Children's Bureau about the high baby death rate where wages are low and families too large. His answer was that statistics lied and he "wouldn't read 'em." He scoffed at the idea that children needed a fair chance for education. "This education business is overdone. What children need is work." He countered all facts and all logic with " I decline to argue."

'I WILL NOT.'

On being invited to read a booklet giving the main reasons for our measure he replied, "I will not. I don't need to," and he wound up with the stentorian advice, "Young woman, you better go home and pray for a clean heart." But within a day or so he sent us the following note:

"My Dear — :

"... Perhaps I was a little hasty with you when you called that morning. You took me somewhat by surprise. If you should happen over this way again, and could catch me when I am not very busy, I should be glad to talk over matters with you more fully, and get your viewpoint more clearly. Yours very truly, — ."

And, lo! the next time he was gentle and receptive. He chuckled over the query as to whether the farmers in his State sowed wheat as thick as the soil would hold it, and whether they planted potatoes four inches apart or over two feet apart, and if babies didn't need space just like crops. He answered, "That's so, that's so," and presently he was advising us to get the Health Committee to commend the bill to the Judiciary Committee, which would undoubtedly act on the advice.

Our next most spontaneous and unique antagonist was one of the leading orators of the Senate, who delivered this little speech on the mere sight of our card bearing the name "Voluntary Parenthood League": "All these leagues and welfare organizations, no matter how fair they look on the outside or how well they speak or write, are all 'Bolsheviks' at heart, and what they really want is to overthrow the Government of the United States." The mild suggestion that it might be rash to generalize brought a smile and the remark, "Why, yes, that's fair," and he pocketed the offered literature and promised to "investigate."

Speaking of "Bolshevism," here is another item from the interview notebook:

M. W. D. — "Can the country expect level-headed citizenship from the man whose maximum wage isn't over $20 a week, and whose family has increased annually for several years, whose wife is sick, and whose babies are hungry and ailing?"

Congressman X. — "No, certainly not. Those men get desperate. They are ready to take up with any wild ideas."

AND HE BEGGED OFF.

It was just this point of view, plus the unemployment situation, which led one of the foremost conservatives of the Senate to consider for three weeks the sponsoring of our bill. He became convinced that "when father is out of a job is no time for mother to have a baby," and while he felt concerned that the rich don't have more children, he thought that was no excuse for victimizing the poor by laws which try to keep them ignorant as to family regulation. However, he begged off from shouldering the bill, saying that he couldn't undertake it for so long that in fairness to us we should ask someone else to introduce it. He was the fourteenth Senator asked, and by that time the always sympathetic Chairman of the Health Committee said we reminded him of Diogenes, except that instead of hunting for an honest man we were merely hunting for a courageous man!

An outstanding independent of the Senate, one of the truly "busy" members, frankly explained what ailed most of them. "Congressmen are such cowards," said he. "Believe in it? Of course they do, and privately they will all say so, but that's mighty different from sponsoring the bill. I know. I've been here twelve years."

Very few Congressmen have even the partial excuse of belonging to a church which disapproves the scientific control of parenthood. In this connection it is interesting to note that a Catholic member who began by saying, "Even if I had no religion at all I should oppose your outrageous idea," ended by asking for our literature and admitting he was relieved to find that we did not seem to be as he had thought, an immoral lot who were assaulting marriage and the home; and he recognized the fact that our proposed change in the law was merely to make access to information legal, not to compel people to use it, and that therefore the change would not be an intrusion upon any one's religious faith.

A Catholic Congressman from an industrial district crowded with mill workers, listened soberly to the figures of the baby death rate in his home town (130 per 1,000 as compared with New Zealand's world record of 51 per 1,000). The conversation went about like this: "Suppose we look at this thing practically. Do any mills in your district raise a man's wages every time he has a new baby?" "No." "Do you see any legislation ahead that will put wages on that basis?" "I do not." "Don't most mill workers reach their maximum wage at about the age of 80?" "I should say so." "Is it fair then for the Government to deprive these fathers of the knowledge by which they can keep their families somewhere near in proportion to their wages?" He looked pained and said: "It is surely a serious question. I want to think it over."

They have been thinking it over ever since, but, the sponsor is yet to be found.

A NEW TRAIL.

Last August we started an entirely new trail, namely, to take the question to Postmaster General Hays. It was a most fitting move, as Mr. Hays had made public announcement that he did not believe the Post Office should operate as a censorship system, and the present law regarding circulating contraceptive knowledge (Section 211 of the Penal Code) is a censorship law, and it applies to the Post Office.

Mr. Hays was cordial and open-minded, and said the proposition was timely, as he had himself about concluded that he ought to ask Congress to revise all the laws bearing on Post Office censorship. He asked us for a résumé of pertinent data, also for samples of good books by scientific authorities, such as are circulated abroad. On being told that it would break the law (Section 211) to mail such books to him, he said: "Oh, no; I don't want to do that; don't mail them, use the express."

"Can't be done," we answered, "because Section 245 forbids that also." "Well, then, by messenger," and it was done forthwith.

Since then Mr. Hays has been the recipient of all manner of messages from representative people all over the country, who have urged him to make this sensible request of Congress. They have reminded him that our measure does not ask Congress for any appropriation (a great asset in these times when taxpayers are rebellious), that it has nothing to do with political partisanships, that it is a great service to health, that it will remove a peculiarly offensive type of censorship, and will do honor both to the country and to him. Particular attention has been called to the fact that the proposed measure provides not only for removing the words "preventing conception" from the obscenity statute, but that a new provision is added to the law providing that

> *no printed information as to methods of preventing conception, and no ingredients compounded for the purpose of preventing conception shall be transportable through the mails or by any other public carrier in the United States except such as bear endorsement of duly licensed physicians or public health authorities.*

This latter provision is to guard the public against unhealthful, fraudulent or purely commercial methods.

This Federal act will not only make published information transportable all over the country, but in twenty-four States, with a population of over 46,000,000 people, physicians may begin at once to teach the control of conception in their private practice and in all the clinics, hospitals, dispensaries and the various health centres. It will lift the birth control movement quite beyond the agitational stage; and that is just what the Voluntary Parenthood League wants.

The Postmaster General's unprecedented opportunity for great service is well put by Mrs. Charles McCasland of St. Louis, who recently wrote to him:

> *It is in your power before you leave office as Postmaster General, unhampered by any political consequences, to do one great act of service to the people of the United States which will make your name and your career remembered forever with gratitude. ... Mr. Hays, by one quiet statement you have the power to set in motion the undoing of this great wrong. You have the power. Will you also have the glory?*

Control of Population.

BY THE NEW YORK TIMES | MAY 15, 1925

URGED BY MRS. SANGER to present his case against birth control, Dr. Louis I. Dublin delivered an address of peculiar acumen and persuasiveness, the text of which is now made public. Admitting the high importance of the subject and the need of frank and full discussion, he contends that the league has based its propaganda on "an emotional reaction" and not on a "scientific analysis"; that it has studied only a single phase of a situation which is governed by widespread economic and social forces, and has taken a narrowly individualistic view of a problem more vital than any other to the welfare and permanence of the nation. His own conclusion, based on studies made as statistician of the Metropolitan Life Insurance Company, is that the proper field of birth control is limited to the shiftless poor and requires a wiser and more scientific administration than it has received.

Present evidences of an increase in our population are "spurious and misleading." They result from the huge immigration of the recent past and the fecundity of our foreign population of the first generation. Even under present restrictions, immigrants "pad" statistics, being mainly "at the reproductive ages." There are more births and fewer deaths per thousand than there would be if all our people had been long subject to American conditions. Except for the "padding from without," the present birth rate of 23 per thousand would fall to 20 per thousand, and the present death rate of "a little over 12" would rise to "well over 15." The rate of increase in population, which is now over 1 per cent a year, would fall to the alarming figure of "one-half of 1 per cent." The actual birth rate, moreover, is declining steadily. In the past thirty years, in spite of the hordes of immigrants, it has fallen over 30 per cent. With immigration restricted, the decline will be accelerated. Clearly, our population is in no danger of pressing perilously upon the possible food supply. A thoroughly conservative estimate, corroborated by a calculation made by Professor Pearl on biological grounds, places the period at which our population will have doubled at something like a century and a quarter. Under scientific and intensive culture our land is said to be capable of supporting four times the present population.

Even more impressive are statistics studied from the point of view of the family. Applying the rates of marriage and mortality that prevailed in 1920, every ten couples must have twenty-six children if the population is to be kept even stationary. But one marriage in every six is either sterile or voluntarily childless. Thus couples that do have children must have on the average a fraction over three each, all groups of urban American families recently examined have shown fewer children than this minimum. In rural districts the birth rate slightly exceeds three per family, but is apparently declining. In the Middle West, according to statistics gathered by Professors Barber and Ross, middle class families have shrunk in the present generation from 5.4 children to 3.3. Under American conditions only the shiftless poor tend to multiply, "increasing the proportion of defective and dependent stock."

In conclusion Dr. Dublin calls upon the Birth Control League for "a well-balanced theory of parenthood." Heretofore, he says, "you have limited yourselves almost entirely to arousing sympathy for those who have suffered from over-large families; today you might very well help arouse public sentiment in favor of fairly good-sized families among the rank and file of normal people."

Finds Birth Control Wrecking Home Life

BY THE NEW YORK TIMES | JUNE 10, 1930

NEW YORK STATE Supreme Court Justice Harry F. Lewis said in a statement issued yesterday in his chambers that he deplored the apparent inroads of birth control propaganda in Brooklyn.

He also asserted that there was an "almost complete absence of real home life today in Brooklyn," ascribing this condition to "childless homes." "Birth control information," he said, "may have its good points but can truly be indicted on many counts, the least of which will be responsibility for unhappy marriages and a falling off in the census."

In sixty-four undefended divorce cases tried before him in one day he found that there was only one child for every two families, and that the duration of each marriage averaged less than three years.

"Not long ago a home meant something," Justice Lewis said. "It was the location of our birth. It was the place where we entertained our friends and where we held all our family functions. Today we are born in hospitals, we entertain in our clubs, we eat in restaurants, we entertain our visiting friends in cab-parlors. I cannot help but reach the conclusion that if our Brooklyn women had children there would be more happiness and fewer divorces.

"Presence of children attracts the husband to his home and keeps the mothers from the gossiping neighbors and bridge parties. Absence of children promotes discord. Their presence makes for harmony."

Birth Control Ban Fought by Doctors

SPECIAL TO THE NEW YORK TIMES | FEB. 14, 1931

WASHINGTON, FEB. 13. — Exemption of licensed medical authorities from the provisions of Federal laws which forbid circulation of birth control information was urged before a subcommittee of the Senate Judiciary Committee today by a delegation of scientists, churchmen and others, headed by Mrs. Margaret Sanger. In the delegation were Professor Henry Pratt Fairchild, Professor of Sociology at New York University; the Rev. Charles Francis Potter and Dr. Sydney E. Goldstein of New York; Dr. J. Whitridge Williams, Professor of Obstetrics at Johns Hopkins; and Professor Roswell H. Johnson of the University of Pittsburgh.

An audience which crowded the committee room and overflowed to the corridor outside, applauded the arguments presented by each speaker against the inclusion of the subject of contraception in the "obscenity statutes."

"This law, in effect since 1873," Mrs. Sanger told the committee, "has been responsible, directly and indirectly, for the deaths of approximately 1,500,000 mothers and for the deaths of approximately 15,000,000 children, many of whom were born unwanted and in conditions of hardship, poverty, cruelty and disease."

CONTROL URGED AS PEACE MEASURE.

All the witnesses urged enactment of the bill introduced by Senator Gillett of Massachusetts, which would put contraception in the hands of the medical profession, where, they contended, it rightfully belonged.

They agreed with the introductory statement of Mrs. Thomas N. Hepburn of Hartford, that "the question of birth control is at the bottom of all prevailing social ills, including poverty and unemployment."

Declaring that "the bird of war is not the eagle, but the stork," Dr. Potter, founder of the First Humanist Society of New York, advocated birth control as a peace measure.

"Nations," he told the committee, "expand beyond the ability of their own land to sustain, and the result is war. The practice of birth control enables a country to limit its population to the size indicated by its natural resources and the best health and welfare of its citizens."

Dr. Potter said that among the reasons for "the marked increase in sentiment in favor of birth control, not only on the part of the general public, as indicated by the rapid growth of the number of birth-control clinics, but also among moral and spiritual leaders," were what he said were its beneficial effects on the family, the community and the race.

"Birth control, enabling the proper spacing of children, is better for the child and for the mother," he said, "and also for the father, who frequently is left out of discussions of this subject."

DOCTORS' RESPONSIBILITY CITED.

Forty years' experience, Dr. Williams said, had left him each year more firmly convinced of the importance of supplying women with contraceptive information.

As a result of the restrictions to which the medical profession had been subjected, he told the committee, "there is a huge bootleg trade in contraceptives."

Accurate and competent advice in regard to birth control, he said, "would save the lives of thousands of women, and a doctor who has this information and does not give it incurs a terrible responsibility."

Dr. Johnson said birth control already was being practiced generally among people of the "upper classes."

Dr. Goldstein, New York, representing the Jewish Institute of Religion, said:

"Birth control will not, as so many feel, produce race suicide. The population is not made up of those who are born but of those that survive. I have made a study of the families of doctors, lawyers, clergymen and even legislators, in which birth control is practiced, and the standard of morality is not lower, but, on the contrary, it is higher."

He remarked that the biblical injunction "to increase and multiply" was given at a time when Adam and Eve were the only persons on earth and again after the flood when there were only eight persons alive in the world.

Mrs. Douglas Moffatt of New York, representing the Junior League of that city, said her organization was "overwhelmingly in favor" of the Gillett bill. "Our work in settlements and hospitals of New York," she said, "has shown us that control of the birth rate by this means is absolutely necessary."

Birth Control Peril to Race, Says Osborn

BY THE NEW YORK TIMES | AUG. 23, 1932

BIRTH SELECTION RATHER than birth control as the best means for the improvement of the human race was advocated last night by Professor Henry Fairfield Osborn, in a prepared address read for him by Dr. William K. Gregory of the American Museum of Natural History, before a distinguished gathering of scientists from many parts of the world, during the general assembly of the Third International Congress of Eugenics. The congress opened here yesterday morning at the museum and will continue until tomorrow night.

Dr. Osborn was unable to deliver the address in person, being detained on a scientific trip to the West.

Birth control, Dr. Osborn said, is a negative rather than a positive factor in human betterment. Even if all classes could be persuaded to practice it equally, its effects would at best be only neutral. At present its effects are distinctly bad, since the ablest and most intelligent are the ones who practice it, while the least fit do not. If not checked, he added, it may in the end prove a double-edged sword, eliminating alike the fit and the unfit.

Analyzing the present world crisis, from observations on a recent tour around the world, Dr. Osborn said the situation resolved itself into six "overs" — overdestruction of natural resources; overmechanization of industry; overconstruction of means of transport; overproduction of food and other commodities; overconfidence in future demand and supply; and overpopulation, with consequent permanent unemployment for the least fitted.

'THE ONLY PERMANENT REMEDY.'

"Prisons, reformatories, asylums, great public financial offerings, great national and local appropriations, great tides of human kindness

LIBRARY OF CONGRESS PRINTS AND PHOTOGRAPHS DIVISION

Professor Henry Fairfield Osborn with his wife.

and generosity are merely palliatives, and temporary expedients," Dr. Osborn said. "They may for a time gloss over the cataclysm; they cannot permanently cure it or avoid its recurrence.

"The only permanent remedy is the improvement and uplift of the character of the human race through prolonged and intelligent and humane birth selection aided by humane birth control. This is the keynote of our Third Congress."

Discussing the reality of overpopulation, Dr. Osborn said that even the lives sacrificed in the World War are entirely negligible compared with the natural increase of mankind when no longer checked by disease, by infant mortality and by internecine wars. The International Statistical Institute estimates that the world added 125,550,000 to its total population in the years 1920-1928.

"Birth selection, as distinguished, from birth control," Dr. Osborn continued, *is known as 'positive eugenics,' of which eugenically administered birth control should be only a subsidiary 'negative' principle. As conceived by Galton it is a positive force in the uplifting of society as a whole by improving human quality as distinguished from human quantity.*

It aids and encourages the survival and multiplication of the fittest; indirectly it would check and discourage the multiplication of the unfittest. As to the latter, in the United States alone it is widely recognized that there are millions of people who are acting as dragnets or sheet anchors on the progress of the ship of State. Some radicals propose that they should all be sterilized so as to inhibit the multiplication of their kind. This would be the negative or birth-control method of birth selection.

'A TWO-EDGED SWORD.'

Birth control, primarily designed to prevent the overpopulation of the unfittest or dysgenic, may prove to be a two-edged sword, eliminating alike the fittest and the unfittest. Whatever its benefits in limiting the unfittest, birth control is always in danger still more of limiting the fittest and thus becoming positively dysgenic or against the interests of the race as a whole in which it is practiced. I have in mind the French, among whom birth control has been practiced in the upper classes for centuries, with disastrous racial results. My doubts about the present propaganda and purpose of the birth-control movement are that they are so largely negative and death-dealing rather than positive and birth-encouraging.

Only by some wise and selective means of limiting the number of births can the world find a solution for its disturbed economics. I return from a tour around the world more impressed than ever with the principle of 'not more but better and finer representatives of every race.' I hold that true for America as well as for foreign stocks.

For the time at least I am very doubtful about birth control. In fact, on eugenic as well as on evolutionary lines, I am strongly opposed to many directions which the birth-control movement is taking, chiefly because I believe them to be fundamentally unnatural and hence destined sooner or later to fail of their original more or less benevolent purposes.

Finally, it must be clearly understood that we eugenists are chiefly concerned with birth selection measures which go to improve the general physical, moral and intellectual qualities of mankind, while measures which are designed to serve personal, individual ends and more or less temporary social demands are outside our province. Positive eugenics strive to improve racial quality on the one hand by increasing breeding and offspring among the eugenic element, and on the other negative eugenics by diminishing breeding and offspring among the dysgenic element.

WHAT THE EUGENIC ELEMENT IS.

The eugenic element of the population includes that portion which is able to exert the greater amount of physical and mental energy, by so doing the better to pull its own weight in the social group, and through a superior moral, temperamental and intellectual endowment to make the greater contribution to the understanding of human life conditions, to cultural progress and to general racial improvement. It would be a mistake, however, to regard this element as confined to a narrow class of intellectual superiority, fully granting this class to be highly essential. Many diverse abilities and aptitudes are required for the consistent and balanced development of humanity.

In short, the eugenic element of the population may be defined as that portion of existent humanity which is competent to produce the best resultant evolution of the species.

The birth-control propagandists claim to be benefactors of womankind whose great object is to relieve women of unnecessary suffering and unnecessary burdens. The attempt to relieve womankind of what may be termed the prehistoric and historic burden of the female of the species naturally enlists the sympathy both of the individualists of our time, who are ready to support any measure to give women greater freedom of profession and of action, as well as of the sentimentalists, who do not realize that women's share in the hard struggle for the existence of the race is a very essential element in the advance of womankind.

The relief of the struggle for existence pressure from any animal or plant organism is an extremely dangerous experiment, for it may be said without exaggeration that the struggle for existence is the sine qua non of every great human or animal quality.

Campbell recalls the fact that 'The continuance of the race and the quality of the race rests primarily with women. In short, women are more essential to racial survival than men. ... In any woman who possesses valuable traits which she has inherited and which she can pass on to offspring, the disposition to evade this obligation is a manifest racial delinquency. In order that those who are racially minded might more often be saved from what they would later regret as a major error in their lives, it is highly desirable that all intelligent individuals, particularly women, should understand these and other simple biological facts as early as the period of adolescence.'

I owe to Thomas Huxley the two outstanding principles of my own naturalistic philosophy; first, that nothing which is true can be harmful to the body, to the mind or to the soul; second, that whatever is natural in the wondrous and beautiful order of nature cannot be fraught with danger. On the contrary, whatever is unnatural may not be essentially immoral but may be fraught with hidden dangers. Herein lies my general purpose and standpoint with regard to the main subject of this article. Birth-selection is natural; it is in the order of nature. Birth control is not natural and while undoubtedly beneficial and benevolent in its original purpose it is fraught with danger to society at large and threatens rather than insures the upward ascent and evolution of the human race.

THE BIOLOGISTS' RESPONSIBILITY.

Such ascent, it seems to me, is the greatest responsibility with which we biologists and eugenists are charged today.

To begin at home, 'not more but better Americans,' which raises the question, What is an American? recently debated in The New York Times (Jan. 17, 1932) with a number of my distinguished compatriots. The substance of my contention in this symposium was that the 'Simon-pure' American is not hyphenated. He has all the strong and all the weak points of the ancestral Nordic as well as of the more recent Alpine and Mediterranean stocks. He is possessed of certain qualities which make him far inferior to men of other races, an inferiority which he should freely admit and, as far as possible, rectify by education.

He is now suffering severely from birth limitation which is seriously threatening the best strains of old American stock. He therefore needs to thoroughly understand the principles of birth selection rather than the principles of birth control. For him the Third Congress of Eugenics has a peculiar significance, but since the Congress is international it should carry an equally clear and distinctive message to each of the nations represented as well as to each of the primary races of mankind. The slogan 'not more but better Americans' should have its counterpart in every country in the world in which the rising spirit of nationalism and of an entirely natural and reasonable pride should be accompanied by the consciousness that quality rather than quantity is the essential element of progress in every country and in every race.

With such principles in mind, and with the picture of the world suffering acutely from dysgenic reproduction, from the multiplication of the incompetent, and the alarming increase in the power of the criminal class before me. I cannot refrain from expressing my deep conviction that, of all remedial and restorative agencies, the well-understood and well-applied principles of birth selection advocated by Galton, with birth control as a subsidiary principle, stand in the very front rank of progressive civilization.

DISPUTES DUBLIN ON POPULATION.

From his recent voyage around the world and observations in many lands, Professor Osborn continued, he has reached the conclusion that overpopulation and unemployment may be regarded as twin sisters. From this point he finds that the United States is overpopulated at the present time. In this he takes issue with Dr. Louis I. Dublin, third vice-president of the Metropolitan Life Insurance Company, who found that "our exports exceed our imports" and that "we are quite able to feed and house our present population and many more that may be born or come in from abroad in later years."

"I do not agree with Dr. Dublin," Professor Osborn said, "as to the population in the United States, for I think the present unemployment figures represent a condition likely to be in part permanent.

"A recent unemployment estimate, revised by Dr. Dublin on July 30, is as follows:

Germany	5,500,000
France	1,000,000
United States	10,000,000
England	4,000,000
Total	**20,500,000**

"While some highly competent people are unemployed, the mass of unemployment is among the less competent, because in every activity it is the less competent who are first selected for suspension while the few highly competent people are retained because they are still indispensable. In nature these less-fitted individuals would gradually disappear, but in civilization we are keeping them in the community in the hopes that in brighter days they may all find employment. This is only another instance of humane civilization going directly against the order of nature and encouraging the survival of the unfittest."

CATACLYSM FORCES ATTENTION.

In addition to the six general conditions of overproduction, overpopulation, &c., which Professor Osborn found, he discovered, "in many but not in all countries, overspeculation and a consequent overcapitalization, which places an intolerable burden of debt on individuals and communities which at the present outlook there are few means to repay.

"Every port I visited," he continued, "revealed overpopulation, overproduction, and unemployment — whether in the South Seas or in the great cities of Europe and America. Everywhere ports were full of empty vessels. Everywhere the number of employees in all grades was being cut down, and everywhere the world's staples, even rice, stood about in quantities far exceeding the world's demand.

"It has always required a cataclysm to force a natural law upon the attention of man. Cataclysmic plagues of malaria, of typhus, of yellow fever, of tuberculosis, of cancer, forced upon human genius the imminent crisis of discovery, of palliation, of prevention, of cure. So in this world cataclysm of overpopulation, of overmultiplication of the unfit and unintelligent, of the reign of terror of the criminal, of the tragedy of unemployment, eugenics ceases to be the cult of the few pioneers like Galton and Leonard Darwin; it is forced upon our attention. Once more man is humbled because he is suffering from prolonged ignorance or actual defiance of and transgression of the most central and fundamental of all natural laws."

STERILIZATION OF DEFECTIVES.

Sir Bernard Mallet, K. C. B., of London, in a paper on "The Reduction of the Secundity of the Socially Inadequate" stated that "apart from segregation, which is clearly the best method, it is only to sterilization that we can look to limit the fertility of mental defectives and of those families which are our problem; an increase in their family, after the first two or three, is looked upon by the parents as a misfortune, and there is reason to believe that advantage would be willingly taken by married women of facilities for sterilization if offered."

"It is for this reason," Sir Bernard said, "that two years ago the Eugenics Society undertook to advocate the application of sterilization to mental defectives and to persons afflicted with hereditary defects seriously impairing physical or mental health or efficiency; and as it appeared doubtful whether eugenic sterilization was legal in Great Britain, we promoted the introduction of a bill in Parliament to allow voluntary sterilization under certain safeguards.

"It must, unfortunately, be recognized that little progress has yet been made in the solution of the problem of the reduction in the fertility of the undesirable elements in our population. It is, on the contrary, a commonplace that birth control has so far acted dysgenically, by reducing the fertility of the better-endowed strains, while leaving relatively unchanged the birth-rate of those who are less fit for parentage."

The eugenist, Sir Bernard added, is sometimes apt to create class prejudice by an unqualified assumption that the poor are necessarily less well endowed from a racial point of view than the well-to-do.

Dr. E. S. Gosney of Pasadena, in a discussion of Sir Bernard's paper, said that a recent estimate from Germany was that at least 100,000 women were sterilized there in private practice each year and it seemed likely that the number sterilized in private practice in the United States was greater.

MENTAL DISEASE WIDESPREAD.

"The number of socially inadequate people in the United States is appalling," it was asserted in a paper by Dr. J. H. Landman of New York.

> *The total number of patients with mental disease resident in State hospitals has increased from 31,973 in 1880 to 272,527 in 1929. There were 427,125 patients in all the hospitals for nervous and mental patients in 1931.*
>
> *The number of feeble-minded and epileptics under institutional care in 1929 were 64,253. On April 1, 1930, there were 57,084 deaf-mutes and 63,489 blind in our country. The State and Federal prisoners had increased to 116,626 prisoners on Jan. 1, 1929. Prisoners committed during 1931 reached the large figure of 70,966. Paupers in almshouses numbered 78,090 on Jan. 1, 1923.*
>
> *If the present rate continues, and there is no apparent reason for thinking it will not, by 1934 we will have more than 500,000 people in our nervous and mental institutions alone. One out of every 160 people in the United States during 1930 was a patient in an institution for nervous and mental disorders. Families that send a child to an institution for feeble-mindedness average twice as many as those who send a child to the university.*
>
> *In 1928 it was estimated there were 10,000,000 people at large who were socially inadequate. They would include the mentally defective, the criminal, the blind, the deaf, the crippled, the germ-diseased, the degenerative-diseased, and all other dependents. The estimate of the number of insane and mentally defective, according to the Human Betterment Foundation, exceeds 18,000,000 people in the United States.*
>
> *Deep-seated changes are taking place in the quality and quantity of our people. Some of these changes are beneficial; others are detrimental. Statesmen must take heed of these changes and tendencies. Much of it is fraught with danger to the fabric of our country.*

Dr. Jan Sanders of Rotterdam, Holland, in a paper on "Measures to Encourage the Fertility of the Gifted," said that it was impossible to select all gifted persons by intelligence tests. In separating gifted persons from less gifted it is necessary, he said, to take groups of the population in which a relatively large number of able people are found.

The declining birth-rate noticeable in so many parts of the world,

Dr. Sanders declared, is not so much a biological as it is a moral and cultural phenomenon. He suggested several measures that may be helpful in preventing further decline of the birth-rate.

"In the first place," he said, "women should again be won over to the idea of the large family. Nowadays women prefer fashion to children. We must get rid of the idea of feminism in its old form, according to which woman should be man's equal in every respect, professionally, politically and as regards salary.

"The theory of this so-called equality of the sexes is absolutely incorrect, not only physiologically and biologically but also socially and politically. Woman is indeed man's equivalent, but they each have their own particular task to perform in the world. The woman's main duty always has been and always will be the family. The university woman must know, understand and feel that marriage and children represent, after all is said and done, the highest ideal."

ADVANCE IN EUGENICS TOLD.

Dr. Charles B. Davenport of the Cold Spring Harbor station of the Carnegie Institution of Washington, president of the third congress, in his president's address last night summarized some of the advances in eugenics made in the last decade.

"In the first glance," he said, "the inheritance of a lot of normal varying characters has been placed on a Mendelian basis, such as stature, body build, pigmentation of hair and skin, eye color, hand form; also temperament, mental traits and quality of the special senses. Similar progress has been made in studying defects and diseases on a genetic basis.

"One of the greatest advances of this period of research has been the change in attitude of pathologists toward the hereditary factor in disease. We have come a long way from the standpoint of the medical man who said, in effect, tuberculosis is due to the bacillus tuberculosus and that is all there is to it — despite the fact that practically every adult harbors the tubercle bacillus. Rather the conclusion of Professor

Jobling of the College of Physicians and Surgeons in this city is being reached, who said: "Henceforth the physician and geneticist must work together."

Dr. Theodore Russell Robie of the Essex County Mental Hygiene Clinic declared that poor heredity was the greatest single cause of mental deficiency (50 to 65 per cent), and cited the case of two feeble-minded American families, the offspring of which ultimately cost the government a total of $2,000,000 annually, although at the beginning they could have been sterilized for $150.

The seemingly insignificant 2 per cent mental deficients, he added, will multiply three and one-half times, while the mentally superior fall off in reproduction. We are, figuratively, sterilizing the fittest as the result of the low reproduction figures for intelligent women, which is one-third that of the other classes.

A $50 monthly bonus by the State to parents of good heredity when their third child reaches the age of 5 was advocated by Dr. Renato Kehl of Rio de Janeiro, Brazil.

Fight Is Renewed on Birth Control

BY THE NEW YORK TIMES | DEC. 23, 1935

BIRTH CONTROL ADVOCATES again were criticised from Catholic pulpits yesterday while a Protestant clergyman suggested in his sermon that the controversy had disclosed "how much the pattern of thought of churchmen has actually changed in the last decade."

The Rev. Cornelius J. Drew, of the New York Apostolate, in his sermon, at high mass at St. Patrick's Cathedral, declared that clergymen who advocate birth control, "mercy" deaths, and other "impudent as well as imprudent" interpretations of the law of God were "prophets of decadence" leading their followers back to paganism.

"Murder and suicide, whether of the individual or the race are clearly and seriously forbidden by the Author of Life," Father Drew declared. "To set aside His law, although for the sake of economic expediency, is never the right of His subjects. Even the State has stronger safeguards for its human laws. Because we have a right to add amendments to the Constitution — and then only after lengthy and deliberate consideration — does it follow that we may determine dispensations from the Decalogue? Neither Jewish nor Christian teaching or tradition ever countenanced such an absurd claim.

"To allow that an appetite exists and is to be exercised for pleasure or that we are justified in defeating its natural consequences is a return to paganism. Strange that these spiritual evolutionists should consider progress a return to a former failure."

Mgr. Fulton J. Sheen of the faculty of Catholic University, Washington, D. C., in his morning sermon at the Roman Catholic Church of the Blessed Sacrament, West Seventy-first Street, said:

"The crisis is not in the moral law. It is in those who break the moral law. There are certain minimum requirements in every profession. Should we not then require that those who preach morality be at least moral themselves?"

Contending that the basis of opinion of the committee of thirteen was comparable to placing violators of any established law in the right against those who obeyed the law, Mgr. Sheen said that he saw the trend toward spiritual unity greatly injured by a "denial of the moral law."

The Rev. John Walter Houck, pastor of Pilgrim Congregational Church, Grand Concourse and 175th Street, the Bronx, commenting on the controversy in his morning sermon, said:

> *The controversy now raging between leaders in the Protestant and Catholic Churches regarding birth control tends to show an observer how much the pattern of thought of churchmen has actually changed in the last decade. The confusion of the terms socialism and communism with Christian concepts seems to place the stress upon temporal betterment, external reformation rather than upon the rebirth of a new attitude toward life on this planet as a whole.*

Birth Control Is Accepted by American Medical Body

BY WILLIAM L. LAURENCE | JUNE 9, 1937

ATLANTIC CITY, JUNE 8. — After a struggle of many years birth control received its first official recognition here today from the American Medical Association, which represents organized medicine in the United States.

The association's house of delegates, supreme court of American medicine, meeting during the association's eighty-eighth annual assembly here this week, adopted today the report of its committee to study contraceptive practices, appointed two years ago, which recommends that the American Medical Association officially approve birth control as having a definite place in medical practice.

The house of delegates adopted two far-reaching recommendations of the committee — first, that the American Medical Association investigate the various forms of contraception with a view to disseminating authoritative information on the subject to the medical profession, and second, that the association promote the teaching of proper methods of birth control in the medical schools.

The action marks another landmark in the annals of American medicine. For many years all efforts to gain official status for birth control, as a legitimate part of medical practice, have been bitterly fought and successfully blocked by powerful groups, religious and otherwise, within the ranks of American medicine.

With the settlement of this issue the house of delegates settled down to give further consideration to the most important problem facing American medicine today, whether to give official recognition to the principle, introduced in a resolution yesterday by the Medical Society of the State of New York, that "the health of the people is the direct concern of government and that a national health policy directed toward all groups of the population be formulated."

This resolution, the adoption of which would mark a distinct turning point in American medical practice, was referred back to committee at the meeting of the house of delegates this afternoon. It will be acted upon at the scheduled meeting Thursday morning.

Meantime, there was evidence of much heated discussion behind the scenes. Tomorrow an all-day "public" hearing will be held by the committee, at which every member of the association will be entitled to express his views on this issue.

The air here is charged with a tenseness never before observed by veteran attendants at annual meetings of the association. Whatever the outcome, every one here realizes that organized medicine in America now stands at the crossroads and that it can no longer champion the status quo as it has done in the past.

BIRTH CONTROL RECOMMENDATIONS

The approved recommendations of the committee on birth control are:

> *That the American Medical Association take such action as may be necessary to make clear to physicians their legal rights in relation to the use of contraceptives.*
>
> *That the American Medical Association undertake the investigation of materials, devices and methods recommended or employed for the prevention of conception, with a view to determining physiologic, chemical and biologic properties and effects, and that the results of such investigations he published for the information of the medical profession.*
>
> *That the Council on Medical Education and Hospitals of the American Medical Association be requested to promote thorough instruction in our medical schools with respect to the various factors pertaining to fertility and sterility, due attention being paid to their positive as well as to their negative aspects.*
>
> *All dispensaries, clinics and similar establishments where information and advice concerning the prevention of conception are given to the public should he under legal licensure and supervision and under medical control.*

The committee on birth control included the following physicians:

Carl Henry Davis of Milwaukee, chairman; George W. Kosmak, New York; W. A. Coventry, Duluth, Minn.; Richard J. O'Shea, Seattle, Wash.; John Rock, Boston; Willard Richardson Cooke, Galveston, Texas; E. D. Plass, Iowa City, Iowa; James R. Bloss, Huntington, W. Va., and W. C. Woodward, Chicago.

The committee was appointed by the board of trustees of the association, pursuant to a resolution adopted by the house of delegates at the annual convention in Atlantic City in June, 1935. It submitted a preliminary report at the convention in Kansas City last year and the committee was authorized "to continue a study of birth control and to report further to the house of delegates."

REPORT LIMITED IN SCOPE

The present report of the committee, it was said in the report, "is limited to a consideration of the prevention of conception only as it refers to the relation of physician and patient."

"Information concerning contraception," the report says,

> *is admittedly available to persons in favorable economic circumstances. There appears to be no law to prevent physicians who work in dispensaries from furnishing patients there with any information that may lawfully be furnished to patients in any other economic group. In all cases the legal justification is the medical need of the patient.*
>
> *In view of the frequent occurrence of medical indications for the prevention of conception, and in view of the medical complications that arise from ill-advised contraceptive practices resorted to by women on their own initiative and without medical advice, which call for medical care, medical students should, in the opinion of your committee, be instructed fully concerning fertility and sterility and taught the clinical considerations and therapeutic application of contraceptive methods.*
>
> *It is recognized that voluntary family limitation is dependent largely on the judgment and wishes of individual parents. The intelligent, voluntary spacing of pregnancies may be desirable for the health and general well-being of mothers and children. This raises the question of how many pregnancies are biologically desirable and physically safe, and of the best practical means for determining the proper interval between them.*

MANY FACTORS TO BE STUDIED

No arbitrary interval can be stated. A variety of factors must be considered, including the patient's general health, the character of the previous pregnancies and labors and of recovery from their effects, and the incidence of intercurrent illness. Your committee reiterates the opinion, expressed in its first report, that each case must he determined by the individual judgments of parents and physician, based on the conditions present.

In its first report your committee stated that it had been unable to find evidence that existing laws, Federal or State, had interfered with any medical advice which a physician felt called on to furnish his patients.

This view has been supported by the recent decision of the United States Circuit Court of Appeals, Second Circuit, Dec. 7, 1936, in U. S. vs. One Package, in which it was held that a statute the words of which forbade absolutely the importation of articles for the prevention of conception was not designed to prevent the importation of things which might intelligently be employed by conscientious and competent physicians to save life or to promote the well-being of patients.

Although the statutes in force in the several States that forbid the dissemination of information concerning methods for the prevention of conception do not in express terms exempt physicians from their operation, it seems fair nevertheless to assume that the State courts, if called on to construe them, will adopt lines of reasoning similar to those followed in the case cited and in other cases decided by United States courts, leaving physicians free to give information concerning contraception when required to meet the medical needs of patients.

RESOLUTION DEMANDS ACTION

What was left unsaid by the committee's official report was supplemented in a resolution presented by Dr. Hans H. Reese of Madison, Wis., on behalf of the American Neurological Association, which is composed of a group of the country's leading neurologists. The resolution reads as follows:

Your committee on contraception, recognizing the important advance that has been made in the physician's use of contraceptives by the decision of the United States Circuit Court of Appeals, desires to present the following resolution:

Whereas, because the aforesaid decision of the United States Circuit Court of Appeals has handed down to the medical profession a bill of rights in the field of contraceptive medicine and because the decision marks the termination of a struggle begun in 1873 to make clear that the Federal Obscenity Laws do not apply to the legitimate activities of the physician, and that he may now prescribe a contraceptive in the interest of life and health.

INROADS OF POPULAR THOUGHT

Therefore be it resolved, that the American Neurological Association urge the American Medical Association again to consider seriously the inroads that are being made on the prestige of organized medicine by the rapid advance of popular thought in the matter of social medical science, as evinced by the success of lay organizations in carrying out their program for greater freedom in the matter of contraception.

It has come to the pass at which the road for medical advance is blazed by laymen, assisted by the law. Unless organized medicine is directed by far-seeing and free-thinking leaders, untrammeled by the aged and antiquated fetters of sophism, it will most certainly come to pass that organized medicine will in the not-distant future come entirely under the control of lay and legal administration, assisted by their political allies.

The American Medical Association is further urged to take up at once the matter of proper teaching of contraception at the medical schools and the organization of medically supervised contraceptive clinics in the hospitals. The time has passed for discussion and debate. The fact remains that the physician is now free to use contraceptives in his practice and should be educated in their use.

A resolution introduced by Dr. McLain Rogers of Oklahoma requested the board of trustees "to procure through the United States Government an investigation by some unbiased, qualified agency of the pretension of osteopathy and of other alleged healing cults."

The annual ceremonies of installing the president-elect in office were held tonight at a gathering of several thousand physicians in Convention Hall. The president-elect, Dr. J. H. J. Upham of Columbus,

Ohio, delivered his inaugural address on "The Advancement of Medical Education" following the address of the retiring president, Dr. Charles Gordon Heyd of New York, on "Professional Freedom and Social Responsibility."

Dr. Heyd, after picturing the medical situation as it is today, said:

"We are slowly developing a society in which old age with its degenerative conditions will represent a constantly increasing percentage of disease. The United States by 1960 may have a stationary population.

"One out of four or five of the population will be over 60 years of age, and heart disease, cancer, nephritis, pneumonia, accidents and apoplexy will move up as the chief causes of death. Medical practice will require a more personal service, a more extensive control, and, I believe, will require more physicians to take care of them."

Dr. Upham urged the physicians to keep up with advances in medicine by post-graduate medical education, reading of medical publications and attendance at medical conventions. He warned of the possibility that should the physicians fail to keep abreast of the times the various States might take action by calling for re-examinations at certain intervals.

Freer Data Urged on Birth Control

BY WINIFRED MALLON | APRIL 13, 1938

CHAPEL HILL, N.C., APRIL 12. — What America needs is a thorough survey, biologically and socially, of its human resources, Dr. Norman E. Himes, Professor of Sociology at Colgate University, declared in an address tonight before the Conference on Conservation of Marriage and the Family, which opened to-day at the University of North Carolina.

"Such a survey need not be a pious elaboration of the obvious," he said. "A beginning already has been made in the reports of the National Resources Committee, which should be published in full, but, instead, these reports are being shelved, if not actually suppressed, by government officials because they contain political dynamite and because they occasionally mention the subject of birth control."

Suppression of the reports was charged by Hr. Himes, and an appeal for their publication was made during a historical review of "Birth Control Through the Ages."

Dr. Himes told the conferees, including experts in the social sciences from all parts of the country, that in this matter the United States was only now "beginning to catch up with the Greeks."

URGES 'ADULT ATTITUDE'

He urged the importance and necessity of an "adult attitude toward, and democratic instruction in, scientific methods of birth control."

"Though birth control is now accepted in principle by the majority of the American people, there are still many who need more scientific instruction," Dr. Himes said. "Since our 400 clinics reach only a small proportion of the population, we need to develop special services for rural areas and to turn birth control over to the public health officials. Only as instruction is democratized can we reverse the present dysgenic trend.

"America urgently needs a biological plan. If it would spend the price of one battleship, say $100,000,000, for a ten-year biological and sociological survey of the human resources of the United States, we might know much more than we now do about the biological implications of present population trends.

"We know that the wrong family stocks are now doing most of the reproducing. One-half of the next generation is being produced by one-third of the population, and this is the poorer, socially disadvantaged part which is unable to give its children average advantages for education and cultural advance.

"Present reproductive trends point to a possible decline in the intelligence of the American people, amounting to approximately two or three per cent. If such is ultimately proved to be the case by further research, its implications for a democratic society are far-reaching.

APPROVES A. M. A. ACTION

The American Medical Association in endorsing recently in its annual convention the medical importance of birth control has "at last caught up with the Greek physicians who took for granted the prevention of conception in certain medical cases," Dr. Himes said.

Information on such methods should be freely disseminated among adults, Hr. Himes argued, "because any other policy is inconsistent with the principles of human liberty and because such instruction is needed not only to preserve health and to keep families from sinking into dependency, but to save the very lives of mothers."

Asserting that birth control, wisely directed, is "one of the greatest forces for social, economic and racial regeneration that man has succeeded in wresting from nature," Dr. Himes warned those who think the current interest in it ephemeral that they delude themselves.

Dr. Ernest R. Groves, founder and director of the pioneer course now in its fifteenth year at the University of North Carolina, in his opening address this morning, joined Hr. Himes in his views on the question.

Both emphasized the historical approach and sociological significance of the academic programs of instruction in preparation for marriage, which they said were designed to "help young people carry out their highest desires" not only for personal happiness in their married lives but for development into socially mature and effective members of their communities.

The methods of teaching preparation for marriage to college youth were discussed in a "question and answer" period concluding the morning session, and in a roundtable discussion this afternoon, led by Dr. O. T. Binkley of the University of North Carolina.

Members of the conference were the guests at luncheon of the faculty of Duke University, several of whom cooperate as specialist advisers with Dr. Groves and Dr. Binkley in the teaching here.

Dr. Himes's lecture tonight was followed by a reception for the delegates and guests.

CHAPTER 3

War and Change

After the end of World War II in 1945, advocates for birth control once again gained momentum. Doctors and birth control activists argued that, in the post-war "baby boom," it was important for women to have access to information about birth control. There was also more time and money to be dedicated to birth control research, and important developments were made in discovering chemical compounds that could be used for a birth control pill.

Birth Spacing Seen as Post-War Need

BY THE NEW YORK TIMES | JAN. 22, 1947

POST-WAR PROBLEMS of veterans and their families have created a new need for planned parenthood information, Dr. Abraham Stone, a vice president of the Planned Parenthood Federation of America, declared yesterday. He spoke at the opening of the federation's two-day twenty-sixth annual meeting in the Hotel Roosevelt. Two hundred and fifty delegates represent 206 local committees and thirty-eight State leagues.

Veterans' wives, many accompanied by their husbands, are frequenting federation centers to "seek advice on postponing additions to their families while living under crowded conditions with in-laws and other relatives," Dr. Stone said.

Another angle of the veteran problem approached by Dr. Stone was the large number of former GI's attending college while their wives took jobs. These couples find it unwise to bring up a family under such circumstances, he said. He suggested that marriage counseling be emphasized more in the organization's centers. Asserting "too few hospitals" have fertility services, he also urged local units of the federation to spur the organization of such clinics "even if we have to aid in subsidizing them."

CHILDLESS ASK HELP

D. Kenneth Rose, national director of the federation, reported that 50 percent of appeals for help received by local leagues came from childless couples.

Progress achieved in State leagues was outlined in a series of reports by their presidents. Particular interest centered on the reports of Mrs. Walter Davenport of Winsted, Conn., and Mrs. Walter E. Campbell of Boston, who represented two States where supplying information on birth control is still illegal. Both predicted that the legislation would be repealed.

Mrs. Davenport said that "for the first time, thanks to the election of an overwhelming Republican Legislature, Connecticut has a chance to repeal the old law which forbids physicians to give contraceptive advice for any reason."

She reported a "strong committee of 200 physicians formed to present the case to the Legislature," with more than 1,000 Connecticut physicians "endorsing repeal of the old law," and added that this year provided the best chance for Connecticut to give its physicians "freedom to prescribe for their patients as they see fit."

MINISTERS URGED TO ACT

The Rev. Charles A. Engvall minister of the First Unitarian Church of Niagara Falls, N.Y., urged that ministers of free Protestant churches include "some kind of injunction on planned parenthood," which he said should be "gracefully phrased," into marriage and baptismal services. He also advocated that ministers "come out publicly for planned parenthood in sermons, particularly at such appropriate times as Mother's Sunday and Child Health Day on May 1."

Integration of the federation's program into hospitals and public health services was recommended by Dr. Stone and Mr. Rose in the final sessions of the day, with Mr. Rose viewing it as "part of the public health program of the country." Only sixty-nine of 4,400 hospitals in the country have contraceptive clinics, he said.

Dr. Sophia Keegman, medical consultant for the New York State Federation, urged that "public hospitals give to poor people the same medical benefits that rich people can obtain privately." She advocated that public pressure be brought to bear to counteract political pressure which prevented installation of contraceptive clinics in city hospitals.

New Anti-Fertility Compound

BY W. L. L. | APRIL 13, 1958

DRS. SHELDON J. SEGAL and Warren Nelson of the Laboratory of the Population Council, the Rockefeller Institute, New York, reported last week at the annual meeting of the American Association of Anatomists at Buffalo on animal experiments with a new type of anti-fertility compound that has proved itself effective when administered by mouth.

The new oral contraceptive differs in some important respects from other oral anti-fertility compounds developed so far. The latter belong to the group of chemicals known as steroids, namely, the family of vital substances that includes the male and female sex hormones, which play an all-important role in the process of reproduction. The new compound is non-steroid in nature. Whether or not this difference constitutes an advantage remains to be determined.

MODE OF ACTION

The mode of action of the new compound also differs from the mode of action of the present anti-fertility compounds now being tested in Puerto Rico on some 250 women. The latter compounds are synthetic chemicals related to the female sex hormone named progesterone, which nature produces after conception has taken place to prevent further ovulation during the pregnancy period. These synthetic compounds, like their natural cousin, act by suppressing ovulation. This is achieved by their suppression of the ovulation-stimulating hormone secreted by the pituitary gland at the base of the brain.

The new anti-fertility compound appears to act in the fallopian tubes to prevent the descent of the fertilized egg to the womb.

EXPERIMENTAL TESTS

The tests so far have been carried out on rats, and Drs. Segal and Nelson emphasized that no conclusion can as yet be drawn about the possible role of the new substance as an oral anti-fertility factor in human beings.

The new compound, known as MER-25, was given orally to the rats at a dose of 25 milligrams per kilogram of body weight, which is the equivalent of about 1 ¾ grams for a 150-pound human being. When treatment was initiated on the day of mating and continued throughout the normal period during which the egg is implanted, "implantation never occurred," the Rockefeller scientists reported.

Birth Control Issue Again Stirs Debate

BY EDITH EVANS ASBURY | AUG. 24, 1958

THE QUIET BUT stubborn determination of a group of New York physicians to practice the same kind of medicine in public hospitals that they practice in private and teach in the five medical colleges in the city has forced a very controversial issue — birth control — to the unwilling attention of public officials.

So far as the city administration is concerned, the long dormant controversy could not have boiled up at a more inconvenient time. An important election is just around the corner, in which candidates for state and national office may very well suffer from disapproval of blocs of voters over the handling of the question that has arisen in local hospital administration.

Standing firmly against any kind of artificial birth control as immoral for the whole community is the Catholic Church.

On the opposite side are the majority of non-Catholics — among them Protestants, Jews and those with no religious affiliation. They approve of birth control with varying degrees of reservation, but unite in protesting any public policy that bans it for all.

In the middle is the embattled Commissioner of Hospitals, 60-year-old Morris A. Jacobs, a career civil servant, a physician and a Jew. When the issue was posed early this year he tried to dodge it.

BAN IMPOSED

On July 16, Dr. Jacobs moved decisively for the first time. He took an open stand against birth control therapy in city hospitals, and since has maintained this position.

His stand was in reaction to official notice by Dr. Louis M. Hellman that he was going to fit a patient with a contraceptive device at Kings County Hospital, in Brooklyn. Dr. Jacobs ordered Dr. Hellman not to proceed. The patient involved was Protestant and diabetic,

THE NEW YORK TIMES

Commissioner Jacobs.

and had recently borne her third child, the second by Caesarian section.

Dr. Hellman's calculated move was the culmination of a campaign spearheaded through the Academy of Medicine to lift the unwritten but definite ban on contraceptive counselling in city hospitals.

Dr. Hellman obeyed Dr. Jacob's order, but protested publicly that his only alternative was to refer the patient for sterilization as, in his opinion, another pregnancy would endanger her life.

Protestant, Jewish and civic groups protested and issued statements defending birth control on moral, religious, medical and legal grounds. It was also protested that the principle of separation of church and state had been violated. Catholic groups praised Dr. Jacobs, and his position was supported by the Association of Medical Boards of the Department of Hospitals.

Mayor Robert F, Wagner asked the Commissioner for a report. Both he and Dr. Jacobs withheld further comment.

MAYOR'S POSITION

Two weeks after he received Dr. Jacobs' report, Mayor Wagner, in answer to questioning by reporters, said (1) he would not make the report public; (2) he was, as a practicing Catholic, personally opposed to birth control in municipal hospitals; (3) the decision was a medical one, and rested with the Commissioner and the Board of Hospitals.

During the past week it has become apparent that Dr. Jacobs hopes for a compromise solution to his problem where by non-Catholic patients in city hospitals might receive oral advice and be referred to private clinics for contraceptive devices. It is possible, he told reporters, that such referrals are already being made.

Some opponents of Dr. Jacobs' policy concede that such a compromise is the most that can be hoped for, considering the determined stand of the Catholic Church, and the large proportion of Catholics in the city who would object to the use of the taxes they pay for the purchase of devices they consider immoral.

Others protest that the proposed compromise evades the basic issue of providing the same quality of medical care in public hospitals that is available to those able to pay for private care. They insist that contraceptive therapy is a medically approved practice legalized by New York State. To deny it to city patients who need and want it because it is morally objectionable to a particular religious group is a violation of civil rights, this group holds.

Severe critics of Dr. Jacobs accuse him of basing a policy decision on religious pressure and political expediency in a manner unworthy of a public official and a physician.

More sympathetic observers say that as administrator of a large hospital system caring for hundreds of thousands of patients with a variety of very serious ailments, he must protect the other services from disruption that might result among Catholic personnel from institution of birth control service. They also point out that the Commissioner is responsible to a Mayor who has made his personal view on the matter clear.

OTHER GROUPS

Still to be reckoned with are the New York Academy of Medicine, the Hospital Board, and the courts.

The Hospital Board may order him, at its next meeting on Sept. 17, to reverse his policy. It consists of five prominent physicians and five equally prominent laymen in addition to Dr. Jacobs, who is chairman. Only two members of the board are Catholics. One member is an officer of Planned Parenthood. Others are known to be strongly pro-birth control.

The Academy of Medicine, in requesting a definition of policy last winter, informed Dr Jacobs that "contraceptive counselling is part of the practice of medicine" and asked that the Board of Hospitals "place on its agenda the subject of contraceptive counseling in municipal hospitals."

At its next meeting, the Academy will probably take another look at Dr. Jacobs' response to its original query, and ask how his order to Dr. Hellman can be reconciled with this excerpt from it:

> *There shall be no interference in proper and accepted therapeutic practices nor intervention in ethical relationships between patient and physician.*

Progress on Birth Control Pill

BY THE NEW YORK TIMES | JUNE 12, 1959

AT THE PRESENT explosive rate of increase, the world's population is expected to reach a total of more than seven billion in the next hundred years.

A recent study by the International Chamber of Commerce found that population growth in the Far East is outstripping the rise in food production, so that food per capita is less now than before the war. Population experts warn that unless birth-control measures are taken in the near future the explosion of what is described as the "Population Bomb" will prove more dangerous than all the stockpiles of atomic and hydrogen bombs.

BASIC NEEDS

It is generally agreed that the most effective birth-control measure would be the development of a contraceptive that could be taken orally. Such a contraceptive pill must be harmless to the woman taking it and must be low in price. Another quality sought is prolonged effectiveness, so that the taking of one tablet would be sufficient to check fertility for several months.

No such tablet has as yet been developed, but progress toward its achievement is reported in the current issue of *Science* by a team of investigators headed by Dr. Gregory Pincus of the Worcester Foundation for Experimental Biology, Shrewsbury, Mass.

Dr. Pincus and his associates report on the use of an oral contraceptive by 830 women in Puerto Rico and Haiti over a time interval covering, for the group, 8,113 menstrual cycles. The tablet is a combination of two synthetic relatives of female hormones. One, a relative of progesterone, suppresses ovulation, the production of the egg from which all life begins. The other induces an artificial menstrual cycle. The tablet is taken daily from the fifth to the twenty-fifth day of the cycle.

The data show, the report states, a 96 percent reduction from the pretreatment rate of pregnancies. "It is clear," it adds, "that if the regimen is followed faithfully, practically a 100 percent contraception occurs; it is also clear that the rate of conception is proportional to the number of tablets missed."

THE ADVANTAGES

The method, the report states, is (1) effective; (2) does not cause any significant abnormalities in the menstrual cycle; (3) does not adversely affect the reproductive tract and its adjuncts; (4) does not have adverse physiological effect in general; (5) does not adversely affect the sex life of the subjects; (6) does not impair fertility upon cessation; (7) can be used in low doses.

However, one of the major drawbacks is that the present cost of each tablet is 60 cents. This is much too expensive for the populations that have the highest birth rates.

Mother Sees Gain in Sterilization

BY DAVID BINDER | SEPT. 13, 1962

WARRENTON, VA., SEPT. 12 — Mrs. M. is a Negro woman old before her years. She has eight children and she works five days a week as a maid to support them.

At 32 she looks ten years older. Her gentle face is lined by fatigue and her dark eyes are lusterless. She and her husband, an alcoholic recently released from jail, are separated.

Her situation today is not much different from what it was two years ago, but according to Mrs. M., a native of Fauquier County, there has been one change that has helped her to face the future with more confidence.

Eighteen months ago she asked to be sterilized at the Fauquier Hospital's maternity clinic in Warrentown. The operation was performed following payment of a $1.50 fee under a program established to aid indigent mothers. "I feel better for it," she told a visitor.

PROGRAM STIRS FUROR

The sterilization procedure, which was requested by sixty-three of the 201 women who have asked maternity care since the clinic started, has caused a nation-wide uproar during the last eleven days.

It has been denounced by prominent clergymen, editors and politicians, most of them outside Virginia.

In an interview Mrs. M. said she was unaware of the controversy.

It was well after sundown and she had just returned from a town thirty miles away. She had driven there at 6 A. M. to work. Now her hair was askew and she was plainly exhausted.

Her home is a former general store on Baldwin Ridge, one of the foothills of the Blue Ridge Mountains where Confederate signalmen relayed troop movement messages prior to the Battle of Bull Run 100 years ago. The wooden walls are unpainted and the cold tile floor has no rugs.

EXPLAINS DECISION

Bright-eyed children romped in the living room — more than a dozen of them, belonging to Mrs. M., her sister-in-law and several neighbors — Cynthia, Elwood, Michael, Deborah, Carol, Gary, David, Tom, Randolph, Paul, Preston, Jacqueline, Bunkie and three Andrews.

"I make seven dollars a day," Mrs. M. said. "I get up at 5 o'clock and sometimes I don't get home till 10. My husband is supposed to pay $30 a week support for the kids, but he's only paid three times."

Asked why she had chosen to be sterilized, Mrs. M. said:

"I did it because my husband is an alcoholic, because I was getting sick every time I was with a child. The doctor said it comes from having so many children so close together, eleven months apart.

"If I went to work I couldn't stay because I had to take care of the kids. I wanted to be so I couldn't have kids. Eight was more than I could take care of."

Mrs. M explained that she had heard about the free clinic at Fauquier Hospital from her father-in-law. During her first visit volunteer aides explained birth control to her, including various contraceptive methods as well as sterilization. She chose sterilization.

"I was five or six months along with my eighth child," she said, "and I was getting such bad attacks of asthma that I had to lie on the floor to breathe.

"I and my husband talked it over and he agreed. The second time I went to the clinic he signed the paper with me."

The operation took place a month later and she remained in the hospital a week. "My kids got polio shots and everything free at the clinic," she recalled.

ABOUT HALF ARE NEGROES

About half of the sixty-three women who have asked to be sterilized at the clinic are Negroes, many of them from poor tenant farm families descended from slaves.

The others are indigent whites, also from tenant farmer families.

Incomes for such tenant farmers range from $50 to $75 a month here, but their wages are usually augmented by what are locally called "findings" — supplies of meat, flour and clothing. Few are on county welfare roles.

According to a survey of forty-four sterilized women from the county taken last year by the clinic, forty were "completely satisfied with the results of the operation." Three others were described as "partially satisfied, with reservation." And one said she wasn't sure.

A reporter who interviewed six of the sterilized women this week, three white and three Negro, said all were "glad" they had had the operation.

Birth Control Taboos Are Easing

BY HAROLD M. SCHMECK JR. | NOV. 18, 1962

FIFTY YEARS AGO today Margaret Sanger unfolded a daring new tactic in her long fight for public recognition of birth control.

On Nov. 17, 1912, in *The New York Call*, she began a 13-week series of articles entitled "What Every Girl Should Know." Today, birth control and contraception have achieved public acceptance as important subjects that are legitimate for open discussion.

However, the subjects are still controversial and Mrs. Sanger's fight is far from finished.

Testifying to this is the fact that one of the most active clinics at Bellevue Hospital is not listed on the institution's bulletin boards.

The clinic's purpose is to dispense guidance and prescribe contraceptives for mothers who have a clear medical need for such services.

That it remains unlisted may be partly a gesture of conciliation to a dispute that erupted in the city in 1957 and was settled in 1958. This was the bitter controversy over whether New York City's municipal hospitals should be allowed to provide contraceptive guidance and materials for patients who desired and needed such aid.

Before 1957 they had not done so, although no law forbade the practice.

The Bellevue clinic opened in September, 1958, with one physician, in a single room. Today it has three physicians, the equivalent of seven rooms, according to its director, and a waiting list so large that some patients have to be seen by appointment outside clinic hours.

PATIENTS GIVEN A LECTURE

All advice, services, contraceptive materials or drugs are free. Each patient is given a lecture on all presently accepted methods of contraception. Then, in consultation with a physician, she is allowed to choose among them. Most patients today choose the new contraceptive pills, according to the clinic's director. Rarely is the rhythm method chosen.

The unit is not a birth control clinic in the broad sense of the word. Only mothers who have a clear medical need to avoid further pregnancy are accepted as patients.

Furthermore, each patient must be referred to the unit from one of the other established clinics at Bellevue. Because of this requirement, the clinic seems to have had one unplanned, but most welcome, effect, according to Dr. Hans Lehfeldt, director of the unit.

He said that there was clear evidence that all of the postbirth maternity clinics at Bellevue were being more heavily attended simply because the news had spread that contraceptive guidance was available at a clinic to which one could only be referred by attending the other clinics.

STRICT CRITERIA USED

In line with the directive of the Department of Hospitals in 1958, the criteria governing the clinic's practices are quite strict. In each case, two physicians must certify in writing their medical judgment that the patient needs to defer future pregnancy and should take contraceptive measures.

The patient must certify in writing that she desires the clinic's services. Each patient is advised to consult with her spiritual adviser and her family.

The medical indications cover a fairly broad range, but they must exist. Conditions considered valid reason for contraception include heart disease, high blood pressure, tuberculosis, diabetes and comparable illnesses that would constitute a hazard to the patient's life if she had another pregnancy. Another important indication is the number of children the patient already has and the span of time over which she has had them. The value of adequate spacing between pregnancies is commonly recognized in private practice.

FIRST STUDY IN 1955

"It is my personal feeling," Dr. Lehfeldt declared, "that our patients should have the same standards of care as private patients."

The vigor with which comparable programs are pursued seems to vary considerably among the other municipal hospitals. Not all have set up specific clinics for the purpose. In fact, a senior officer of the Department of Hospitals said that he did not believe that departmental reports identified any such units as separate clinics. They are simply considered part of each hospital's obstetrical and gynecological services, he said.

Until recent years, no reliable figures on national practices in contraception were available, according to Dr. Christopher Tietze, director of research of the National Committee on Maternal Health, which has offices in the New York Academy of Medicine Building, 103d Street and Fifth Avenue.

The first comprehensive study, based on a small nationwide sample of 2,713 white married women, was done in 1955, he said. There have been others since.

The gist of these seems to be that substantially more than three-quarters of all American married couples practice contraception at some time in their married lives.

Analyses of national preferences in contraceptive methods have tended to yield the same distribution, although all such estimates are probably only tentative.

The most widely used method seems to be the common device worn by the man and described in a recent report as "the male sheath."

It has been estimated that, at any given time, the sheath is the current contraceptive method of slightly more than one-quarter of all couples using any method.

Between 5,000,000 and 6,000,000 gross of the devices are manufactured in the United States annually and about one-fifth of them are exported.

OTHER METHODS EXPLAINED

The next most widely used method is the diaphragm — a device worn by the woman to prevent sperm from the male from reaching the upper region of the female reproductive tract. One estimate for current use of this method at any time is slightly less than 25 percent.

The third method in order of utilization is the rhythm method — the only method sanctioned by the Roman Catholic Church. This is estimated at 21 percent of current use. One study places the rhythm method slightly above the diaphragm in percentage of users.

There are many other methods. Fourteen altogether were listed in an early draft of a still-unpublished survey of reproductive system research compiled at the National Institutes of Health, Bethesda, Md.

By a considerable margin the three methods mentioned above are the most widely used, although the new oral contraceptive pills have already had a remarkable effect. Two other methods have also attracted a great deal of recent interest among specialists.

WIDE PRACTICE IS CITED

One is the use, by the woman, of a spermicidal foam applied to the lower portion of the reproductive organ system. Field tests in Puerto Rico have shown highly promising results.

The other method involves insertion of a plastic ring or coil in the uterus. This has the advantage of acting for relatively long periods with no need for attention from the person using it. Basically, this is an old method held in low esteem by the medical profession because of doubts as to its safety. Preliminary research results suggest that modern variants may be much safer.

Studies have shown that any of the most-used methods — such as the sheath, diaphragm or rhythm — are effective in preventing pregnancy if intelligently and carefully used. In practice, however, the oral contraceptive pills have had rates of effectiveness considerably higher than other means except abstinence.

The available evidence seems to indicate that contraception, using one method or another, is widely practiced in the United States and that it is recognized as proper medical practice by a large portion of the medical profession.

Nevertheless, birth control is one topic that still tends to make some public officials reticent and uneasy. It is also true that the laws governing it are full of incongruities and seeming paradoxes.

In Connecticut anyone who uses any kind of contraceptive is committing a crime, but sterilization — which amounts to permanent contraception — has been held legal in case of "medical necessity." About a year ago, a public figure discussing the Connecticut law, said that it "purports to regulate conduct in that most unregulatable of locations, bed."

In Maryland, according to a survey in 1960 of laws on contraception throughout the United States, it is illegal to sell contraceptive devices in slot machines except in places "where alcoholic beverages are sold for consumption on the premises."

STATES STATUTES VARY

In Massachusetts, according to the same survey, the dispensing of contraceptives has been held illegal only if it can be proven that the purchaser did not buy them to prevent disease. And Wisconsin law prohibits a physician from counseling any unmarried woman on contraception.

Despite variously worded laws, however, most states do not actively interfere. The Planned Parenthood Federation of America, the agency most active in this field, considers that only in Connecticut and Massachusetts is there serious interference with birth control or family-planning activities.

Some states have no laws whatsoever concerning this. In several others that do have quite strictly worded statutes, birth control guidance is an integral part of state health department clinic practices.

It seems clear that a principal factor in making the subject of birth control and related matters so sensitive is a difference of belief between the Roman Catholic Church on the one hand and Protestant and Jewish points of view on the other. Although there is a spread of opinion among individuals in all religious groups, Protestant and Jewish opinion has often been arrayed on the side of birth control during controversies while the Catholic opinion has not.

Ironically, however, it was Protestant majorities that passed restrictive laws related to birth control, even though Catholic opinion seems to be keeping them on the books.

The Catholic viewpoint has been most adamant in opposition to abortion and sterilization.

ROMAN CATHOLIC VIEW

In an educational pamphlet published in September with ecclesiastical approval, the Rev. Walter Imbiorski of the Cana Conference of Chicago, said:

"Direct sterilization is wrong because man has no direct dominion over his sexual faculties and cannot sterilize himself without going beyond the limits of his authority. Direct sterilization is contraceptive in its purpose and therefore a basic violation of the generative function."

In Catholic belief this attitude also applies to contraception by any method other than the periodic abstinence of the rhythm method. Indeed, Father Imbiorski was discussing the morality of using the oral contraceptive drugs in the above quotation on sterilization.

The Rev. John C. Knott, director of the Family Life Bureau of the National Catholic Welfare Conference in Washington, said that the church considered the primary objective of marriage to be the procreation and rearing of children. It is recognized, however, he said, that there can be valid reasons for a couple to abstain from having children or to limit intentionally the size of their family.

But, to do this by any "artificial" means is not proper because it usurps God's governing function in the union between man and wife. Father Knott contended.

MORE RESEARCH NEEDED

Father Knott said that further research on human reproduction was certainly needed. He questioned the wisdom of suppressing the much-discussed National Institutes of Health survey in this field. A revised version of the report is expected to be issued soon.

An early draft estimated total financial support for birth control and "closely related" research at about $5,700,000, of which the contribution from Government sources was put at $1,309,000 devoted solely to basic problems of mammalian reproduction. A panel of consultants was quoted as estimating the level of research needs at $12,000,000 yearly.

As persons who have studied it realize, birth and population control constitutes one area of broad significance, but there are two ways of looking at it.

One can think of 50,000,000 new human beings being added yearly to a planet that, in many places, is already crowded and hungry. One can think in more personal terms, of a mother 21 years old who already has six children, not enough to feed them nor enough strength to care for them and no assurance that she will not bear six more before she is a decade older.

Conversely, and this is often lost sight of, one can think of the couple adequately equipped to care for a family and yet unable to bear children.

That a population problem exists is doubted by few intelligent persons. However, at the same time, no one doubts that it will be solved. It always has been in the past. The concern of many thoughtful persons of all faiths, however, is to find, for once in human history some way of dealing with the problem other than leaving it to the traditional, natural safety valves of famine, pestilence and war.

A New Birth Pill Cuts Side Effects

BY JANE E. BRODY | JAN. 20, 1966

A CALIFORNIA DRUG concern has developed a new birth control pill that may be cheaper and easier to take and may have fewer side effects than oral contraceptives now in use.

The new drug, which is not yet on the market, was developed by Syntex Laboratories, Inc. Dr. Harry Rudel, vice president of the concern, has said that the new pill does not interfere with ovulation and therefore "may lead to greater acceptance by religious groups which are presently opposed" to oral contraceptives.

Dr. Rudel described the pill last month at a medical meeting in Salt Lake City. A report of his remarks appears in the current issue of Medical World News, a magazine for doctors.

Officials at Syntex said yesterday they could make no comment about the drug. The company has applied to the Securities and Exchange Commission to sell a block of its stock, and for 40 days company officials may not discuss any activities of the concern that might affect the action of the stock.

OVULATION IS PREVENTED

Birth control pills now on the market combine two synthetic hormones that prevent conception by preventing ovulation when the pills are taken for a prescribed number of days each month.

The Syntex pill consists of only one hormone, progesterone, and is taken once a day every day in about one-fifth the dosage required by other oral contraceptives, the medical magazine said in its report of Dr. Rudel's description.

He said the drug apparently did not interfere with the woman's hormone system. Instead, he said, it appears to create a "hostile climate" to sperm in the woman's cervix, the canal leading to the uterus and Fallopian tubes, where conception normally occurs.

If the hormone system is not affected, the Syntex drug would be expected to produce fewer side effects than other birth control pills, which suppress the hormones that stimulate the ovaries.

IRREGULARITY EFFECT

Dr. Rudel said the new pill's most serious side effect was a four-day or five-day irregularity of the menstrual cycles in 35 per cent of women tested. Other than that, he said, side effects attributable to the pill are "negligible."

In tests on 764 "highly fertile" Mexican women, Dr. Rudel said, the pill prevented pregnancy through 3,779 patient cycles in all but one woman who took the prescribed dosage.

He noted that the irregularity problem might make the Syntex pill less acceptable to American women, who usually prefer to have predictable menstrual cycles. However, he said that tailoring the drug's dosage to each woman might eliminate the problem.

The researcher said that the new pill could be of immediate benefit to women in low economic groups and to natives of underdeveloped countries.

He described the company's ultimate goal as developing a form of the drug that would be effective as a once-a-year injection.

The Pill: Revolution in Birth Control

BY JANE E. BRODY | MAY 31, 1966

SIX YEARS AGO this month a drug appeared on the American scene that was destined to exert a profound effect on the emotional and social life of the nation.

It was The Pill — the first contraceptive both 100 per cent effective and completely independent of the sex act.

The pill was hailed as a scientific dream-come-true, the emancipator of women, the answer to birth control.

While it was none of these entirely, it was all of them in part. Many women were cautious at first, but soon thousands were asking their physicians to prescribe it. As one of them, a mother of three, explained:

"With the pill, we don't have to worry any more."

Today almost six million American women — nearly one-fifth of those of childbearing age — are believed to be using oral contraceptives. And the number grows steadily.

The pill would seem to be here to stay.

For most of its users, it has revolutionized family planning and relieved a traditional source of family tension: the fear of having unwanted children.

With the pill, newlyweds are confident that their first child will not catch them emotionally and financially unprepared. Middle-aged couples are protected against late-in-life accidents. Others have children precisely when they want them.

The pill also is having an impact on birth control among those women who, because of ignorance or poverty, cannot successfully use older contraceptive techniques. There are definite indications that women in poverty-stricken areas can and will use the pill faithfully.

Many sociologists believe that, because the pill can be talked about on a general, impersonal basis, it has helped remove the fetters from discussion of sex and that this freedom will lead to healthier and better informed attitudes toward all aspects of sex.

But it is precisely this free talk that has caused some to fear that Americans are losing too many personal inhibitions and are headed for a general decline of moral standards. Such fears are difficult to substantiate. The limited research done on attitudes and actions of single women indicates that most using the pill have previously used some less effective contraceptive techniques. Others, who started with the pill, were waiting for the right man rather than the right devices.

There is also some concern about the medical implications of the contraceptive pill. For the first time, millions of young, healthy women are taking a powerful drug regularly for long periods primarily for a nonmedical reason. Some doctors fear prolonged use could have serious consequences because oral contraceptives disrupt normal hormone balance.

To better define the risks of prolonged pill use, the Food and Drug Administration's advisory committee on oral contraceptives is expected to recommend in a report next month a study of 30,000 women over a ten-year period.

Basically, the pills now in general use contain man-made versions of two natural female hormones, progesterone and estrogen. These work to prevent ovulation — the release of an egg from the ovaries — normally occurring once a month, about midway between menstrual periods.

ONLY BY PRESCRIPTION

Oral contraceptives are available only by prescription, usually limited to a six-month supply. This is to assure that the woman will return to her doctor every half year for the recommended checkup to detect any possible complications.

The cost of a month's supply ranges from nothing for indigent patients at Planned Parenthood clinics to about $2.50 for private patients.

The woman is instructed to take one pill at about the same time each day for 20 days. Then the pills are stopped, and within three to five days the woman begins to menstruate. On the fifth day of menstruation, the next 20-day pill cycle is begun.

There are eight brands of oral contraceptives now on the American market. They vary in the combination and amounts of active ingredients.

Six brands combine synthetic progesterone and estrogen in each pill. In the two other brands, called "sequentials," the first 15 pills taken in the 20-pill cycle contain only estrogen. The last five are a combination of progesterone and estrogen.

Manufacturers of the sequential maintain that this sequence is more representative of the woman's natural hormone balance. But it has not been proved that the sequentials affect women any differently than the combination pills.

Although both the combination and the sequential pills offer complete protection against pregnancy when taken as prescribed, reports from a World Health Organization committee and others say the sequentials are more likely to fail if one pill is missed.

Remembering to take the pills is sometimes the woman's greatest problem.

One user remarked: "I often find myself taking two or three pills a day because I forget I've already taken one."

To help women remember, manufacturers have produced such ingenious devices as a pill calendar with punch-out pills.

With one calendar, the woman dials a wheel to select a pill for the day of the week. In another device, a pill card refill fits into a slim compact; markers on the card correspond to the day she began menstruating and the day she is to start the pills.

Despite the problem of remembering, personal histories attest to the fact that oral contraceptives offer the desired protection for millions.

For Mrs. Helen B., the pill has restored the sexual happiness and spontaneity she and her husband knew during their first years of marriage.

"We have three children," she said, "and we can't afford any more. I have a job now to help put the children through college, and another pregnancy would ruin our plans. A diaphragm didn't work for us, as the birth of our third child showed.

"After that, I felt we had to limit sexual relations to times of the month when I'm almost certain I won't get pregnant. That's not too often, you know.

"But now with the pills, we don't have to worry any more. It's just great — like a second honeymoon."

For Susan and Marty W., who married while both were students, the pills meant three worry-free years. Now, with degrees in hand and savings in the bank, they are awaiting the birth of their first child.

DISTURBING QUESTIONS

Jean L., a college-educated career girl, used the pills for several years before she married.

"The possibility of pregnancy was the only reason I could see for not sleeping with a man I loved and was thinking of marrying," she said. "With the pills, this possibility was removed."

Attitudes like Miss L.'s raise disturbing questions in the minds of many:

Will the ready availability of a completely effective contraceptive create a moral as well as a birth-control revolution? Will more youngsters, free from the fear of pregnancy, engage in premarital sexual relations? Will more adults, married or single, become promiscuous?

"There is no virtue in morality if we are pure only because we fear being caught," according to Dr. Roger Shimm, dean of instruction at Union Theological Seminary.

Others, who also note that a morality based on fear is no morality at all, believe the existence of the pill will force many persons to search for a higher standard of sexual morality.

CHAPTER 4

A New Era for Birth Control

The first birth control pill, technically known as the combined oral contraceptive pill, was approved by the Food and Drug Administration (F.D.A.) for use in 1960. However, this didn't mean that birth control pills were immediately available to all women. It took the U.S. Supreme Court case Griswold v. Connecticut, in 1965, to allow access to contraception. The ruling overturned a state Comstock Law, arguing that married couples had a "right to marital privacy." It wouldn't be until 1970, however, that unmarried women would have access to the birth control pill.

Birth Pills Termed Still Experimental

BY HAROLD M. SCHMECK JR. | JAN. 16, 1970

WASHINGTON, JAN. 15 — A prominent scientist cautioned today that all doctors prescribing birth-control pills should treat each patient as though she were part of a research project.

Dr. Roy Hertz, of the Population Council and Rockefeller University, said he continued to hold that view a decade after the pills came into use because important safety questions remained unanswered.

At present about 8.5 million American women are believed to be taking the contraceptive drugs that contain synthetic versions of the female hormones estrogen and progesterone.

Government reports have repeatedly called the pill safe for contraceptive use although not entirely without risk. There are differences of opinion among experts concerning the gravity of the risks. These differences were obvious today in testimony before the Monopoly Subcommittee of the Senate Select Committee on Small Business.

Dr. Hertz, a specialist in research on the human reproductive system and those cancers that affect it, said only two things concerning the pills had been substantiated beyond any reasonable doubt. These are the pills' high degree of effectiveness in preventing pregnancy and the pills' ability to cause blood clotting problems. In some instances deaths have resulted from the clots.

In the testimony today, Dr. Hertz expressed concern over the possible danger of cancer in women who use the pills. He said it had been demonstrated that cancers arise in some animals treated with hormones essentially the same as those used in the pills.

In fact, the scientist, who has often expressed concern over the pills' possible relation to cancer, said:

"Estrogens are to breast cancer what fertilizer is to the wheat crop."

He said testing in animals and clinical use of the drugs in human beings continues concomitantly on the presumption that cancers may be detectable sooner in the animals because they have shorter natural life spans.

"The ultimate outcome of this race between dogs, monkeys and women can be anticipated by informed observers only with great apprehension and concern," he said.

The other side of the argument concerning the cancer risk was presented by Dr. Robert W. Kistner of Harvard Medical School, a well-known specialist in research and treatment of illness related to the female reproductive system.

Dr. Kistner said the pill is safer than pregnancy but not safer than continence. He said it is far safer than cigarette smoking.

In animal experiments of which he was a co-author, Dr. Kistner said synthetic equivalents of the progesterones showed a protective effect against a well-known cancer causing chemical.

The doctor said that among patients at the Boston Hospital for Women there had been no detectable increase in the incidence of pre-cancerous conditions of the female cervix between 1964 and 1969 despite the annual increases in the number of patients who were using the contraceptive drugs.

Both Dr. Kistner and Dr. Hertz agreed that more research would be highly desirable on the health effects of the pills. They indicated that to be of value the studies would have to be done on a large scale.

Dr. Kistner said it had been estimated that it would take a four-year followup of 20,000 pill-users in the 20-to-30-year-old age bracket to have a reasonable chance of detecting a two-fold increase in the incidence of breast cancer.

One of the reasons cited by Senator Gaylord Nelson, Democrat of Wisconsin, for calling the hearings on birth control drugs was the question of the manufacturers' performance in telling doctors the true risks involved.

The final witness at today's hearing, Dr. Edmond Kassouf, of Cranford, N. J., presented evidence to show that the drug concerns had consistently underemphasized the known risks.

Dr. Kassouf said manufacturers' pamphlets still in circulation say nothing of the current data on the risk of blood clot problems or other potential hazards.

Panic and Pregnancies Linked to Senate Inquiry on Birth Pill

BY RICHARD D. LYONS | FEB. 25, 1970

WASHINGTON, FEB. 24 — A New York obstetrician told a Congressional subcommittee today that publicity generated by its hearings on hazards of birth control pills had caused "panic" among women using the drug and "dozens of unwanted pregnancies."

Dr. Elizabeth Connell, an associate professor of obstetrics and gynecology at the Columbia College of Physicians and Surgeons, told the Senate Subcommittee on Monopoly that "we are just beginning to see the first of the pregnancies of women who panicked in January, stopped using their pills and did not seek or use another means of birth control."

In an interview, Dr. Connell said:

"We're getting into the dozens, that I know of, and there probably are many more who have stopped using the pill, become pregnant and not come back to our clinics."

Dr. Connell said that she knew of a 14-year-old girl who became pregnant after she stopped using oral contraceptives. The doctor added that New York doctors were performing abortions on women who have had undesired pregnancies since the subcommittee hearings started six weeks ago.

"Women became frightened," said the petite blonde mother of six who testified for two hours, often fending off pointed questions from Senator Gaylord Nelson, Democrat of Wisconsin, the subcommittee chairman.

NELSON EXPLANATION

Senator Nelson insisted that the hearings were intended to call attention to the potential hazard of the use of oral contraceptives and to the need for more information about the use of birth control pills being given to American women.

But as the hearings resumed today political undertones emerged, with Mr. Nelson digging at pro-pill statements, while three Republican subcommittee members challenged anti-pill positions of the six witnesses who testified.

These included Dr. Phillip Ball, of Muncie, Ind., who urged a five-year ban on the use of oral contraceptives because doctors "have been wrong about birth control pills."

Dr. Ball said he has refused to prescribe the pills for four years because of harmful side effects, including psychological changes in the users.

The doctor said that many times a husband would call and say, "Do something about my wife — my God, she's just turned into a bitch." The doctor cited this to illustrate that many women do not know themselves what the effect of the pills are.

EXCHANGES ON DATA

Dr. Francis Kane, a psychiatrist at the University of North Carolina Medical School, and Dr. John R. McCain, an Atlanta obstetrician, both testified that they had seen women who had become extremely psychotic and sometimes suicidal after having used the pill.

Their testimony provoked long exchanges with three subcommittee Republicans, Senator Jacob K. Javits of New York, Senator Robert J. Dole of Kansas, and Senator Mark O. Hatfield of Oregon, over the interpretation of the data that were presented. The total number of cases the two physicians reported that they had personally observed was about two dozen.

Two other witnesses, Dr. Kenneth J. Ryan, chairman of the Department of Reproductive Biology at Case Western Reserve University in Cleveland; and Dr. Paul Meier, a professor of statistics at the University of Chicago, repeated a theme that many subcommittee witnesses had voiced in the past: that not enough is known about the effects of birth control pills to draw solid conclusions about the medical hazards of their use.

Dr. Connell of Columbia expressed the same sentiments, but added that birth control pills should remain on the market because the social, psychological and medical risks of their use outweighed their potential for harm.

Dr. Connell, the first woman to testify at the hearings, declined to state if she had or would take oral contraceptives herself but said she had told a member of her family "if she ever took another pill she would be out of her mind."

"To date these hearings have not made our lives any easier," Dr. Connell said. "I think much of the previous testimony has been rather like a bikini; what it has uncovered has been interesting, but what it has left concealed is vital."

Dr. Connell, who has established and directed birth control clinics in New York, reiterated the beliefs of many leaders of the family planning movement. These are that the pills are not suitable for all women — in fact may be harmful to some — but that oral contraceptives are extremely beneficial to large numbers of women who for various reasons are not able to effectively use other contraceptive methods.

Poll Finds Shift in Views on Pill

SPECIAL TO THE NEW YORK TIMES | MARCH 1, 1970

PRINCETON, N. J., FEB. 28 — The recent hearings on birth control pills have apparently had a profound effect on the views of American women regarding the safety of oral contraceptives, according to the Gallup Poll.

A sample of the nation's female adult population, completed following the hearings that began Jan. 14, shows the weight of opinion 2-to-1 on the side that birth control pills are dangerous to a person's health. These findings represent a near reversal of opinion from that recorded in a survey conducted three years ago.

In addition, more women today than in the earlier survey expressed uncertainty about the safety of birth control pills.

Women in their twenties are somewhat more inclined to say that birth control pills can be used safely than are women in their thirties and forties, the Gallup organization reported; however, the weight of opinion in all age groups is on the side that these pills are unsafe.

College-trained women are more inclined to believe birth control pills are safe than are women with less than college training, the poll found.

A majority of Roman Catholic women (55 percent) believe the pills to be unsafe, according to the poll, compared to 39 percent of Protestant women.

The doctors and other experts who testified at the Senate hearings were divided in their testimony. Some said the pill might be a factor in causing blood clotting, breast cancer, diabetes, sterility, birth of malformed children and long-range damage to future generations.

However, others at the hearings said that "the pill" was safe for most women.

The impact of the well-publicized hearings is also evident in other results obtained in the latest survey.

Only 37 percent of all women interviewed said they would recommend "the pill" to a woman who did not want more children. The comparable figure in the survey three years ago was 53 per cent.

The Senate hearings, while apparently having had marked effect on attitudes toward the safety of birth control pills, seem not to have changed opinions regarding their effectiveness.

In both the latest and the 1967 surveys, 67 percent of women said they thought birth control pills were an effective contraceptive.

To determine the impact of the recent Senate hearings, the same series of questions asked in a January, 1967, Gallup survey were repeated in the latest survey, which was conducted early this month, Feb. 6-9.

A total of 777 adult women were interviewed in person by the Gallup Poll's field workers. The survey covered more than 300 localities across the nation.

To Them, Two Children Are Fine, But Three Crowd the World

BY JUDY KLEMESRUD | JAN. 12, 1971

MRS. SHIRLEY LEWIS raised two fingers in the V-shaped peace sign yesterday and said she had her own meaning for the gesture.

"It means, "Stop at Two,' " the slender, red-haired woman said, smiling.

Mrs. Lewis, who is the wife of a pediatrics intern, was one of four leaders of the New York chapter of Zero Population Growth who met yesterday to talk about the relatively new and rapidly growing population control group.

Almost 30,000 people in 325 chapters throughout the country have joined ZPG since it was founded early in 1969, she said, and most of them sport the group's button: A black-and-white number with the letters "ZPG" sitting on top of what looks like a road map, but is actually a statistical graph.

The graph is supposed to symbolize what will happen if the world's population continues at its present rate (such a population explosion would have dire consequences, ZPG leaders say), or if there is zero population growth (a stabilized population).

"We're not against children or babies at all," said Peter Decks, a 29-year-old investment banker from Tuxedo Park, N.Y., who has been active in the New York chapter since it was founded a year ago. "We're just against more than two."

The four leaders sat around a table in the group's drafty, unimpressive headquarters — a portion of an artist's loft on the eighth floor of 722 Broadway. The walls are decorated with graphs, charts, posters and slogans such as: "Stop at Two," "Make Love, Not Babies," "Smaller Families or Bigger Headaches?" and "Anyone Can Have a Baby. A Baby. A Baby. A Baby. A Baby. Is It Worth Repeating?"

DON HOGAN CHARLES/THE NEW YORK TIMES

Four leaders of the New York chapter of Zero Population Growth, an activist population control group, are, from left, Mrs. Shirley Lewis, Peter Deeks, Bonnie Kirkpatrick and Judy Senderowitz. They urge a two-child limit for families.

"What we're saying is that if people stop at two now, the population will stabilize by the year 2015," said Judy Senderowitz, 28, chairman of the 800-member New York chapter, who works at headquarters full-time without pay. (Surveys show that most couples want three or more children.)

"Even if we continue at our present 1 per cent growth rate, which demographers say is the lowest since the Depression," she added, "our population will still double in 65 years. And that means we will have to double our schools, hospitals, fire departments and social services."

Probably nothing makes ZPG people angrier than to see pictures of large families in advertisements or newspaper and magazine articles. When this happens, ZPG'ers fire off irate letters to the advertising agencies and the publications.

NO DIFFERENCE

"It doesn't make any difference whether the family can support all those children or not," said Bonnie Kirkpatrick, 29, of Manhattan, who has been advocating population control ever since her days at Mount Holyoke, where she and Miss Senderowitz were classmates.

"The fact is," she added, "the society, the world, and the environment can't support them. The open spaces will gradually diminish, and so will the food and water supply. And I'd hate to think about all the pollution."

ZPG was the brainchild of Richard Bowers, a lawyer from Old Mystic, Conn. It has been especially strong on college campuses and on the West Coast, where Dr. Paul Ehrlich, an entomologist at Stanford University and the author of "The Population Bomb," is one of its leading advocates.

Although the ZPG people call their group "the only activist population control movement," about as radical as they've gotten so far is to picket for the repeal of laws restricting contraception, sterilization and abortion. (The New York chapter refers women seeking abortions to the Women's Medical Center, 80 Irving Place.)

SUPPLYING SPEAKERS

Most of their activities are educational and political, such as supplying speakers to groups that want them, passing out leaflets on street corners, participating in ecological fairs, and supporting tax laws that discourage large families.

Mrs. Lewis and Mr. Deeks, the two married members of the group that met yesterday, are childless, but said they and their spouses planned to have "two children and no more." Then if they want more, they plan to adopt — another ZPG position.

ZPG is a nonprofit, volunteer organization that is financed largely by contributions from members. Membership for one year costs $10. More information can be obtained by writing to the New York chapter at Box 259, Village Station, New York City, 10014.

ZPG has not been popular with everyone. Two angry men recently tipped over a table containing ZPG educational material that had been set up in front of the Museum of Natural History. There has also been opposition from those who, for religious reasons, are against any interference with human reproduction.

"Some people feel very offended," Miss Senderowitz said. "They think we're invading into private territory. They feel that nobody has the right to talk about how many kids other people should have."

Mr. Deeks nodded. "We're confronted with thinking that evolved hundreds of years ago, when the only way a man could survive was if he had 10 children to help him do the work," he said. "Trying to change some people's thinking is like saying motherhood and apple pie are not American."

The Fear That Birth Control May Mean 'Genocide'

BY HARRY SCHWARTZ | MAY 2, 1971

CONCERN OVER THE world's population explosion, and the attendant dissemination of birth control devices and the liberalization of abortion laws, have had their effects in the United States: a marked decline in the birth rate. But they have also spawned a growing controversy over the implications of the zero-population-growth movement for racial and ethnic minorities within the nation.

Traditional opposition to birth control measures, of course, has come from the Roman Catholic Church, on moral grounds. The new opponents base their dissent on political and cultural grounds. The position has been articulated most openly by Jews and Negroes.

Since many Jews have been active in the zero population growth movement, observers have been particularly struck by the dissenting views voiced in a recent issue of the magazine Commentary. In a lead article by Milton Himmelfarb and in a column by editor Norman Podhoretz, the magazine asks in effect whether American Jews are not going to eliminate themselves as an important force in the society by their enthusiasm for population control.

THE ARGUMENTS

It has been argued that the birth rate among Jews is lower than that for most other groups, and that any lessening would further decrease the relative size of the group in the society. The statistical evidence for such conclusions, however, is incomplete: there are, for example, no comprehensive census statistics on the trend over time of births, deaths and contraceptive use among Jews.

The opposition to zero population growth among Negroes has been more widespread.

At the extreme, militants charge that efforts to persuade black women to use contraceptives or to have abortions — where they are legally available — are really aimed at achieving black genocide.

A recent report by a black researcher, Dr. William A. Darity of Amherst, Mass., suggests that these sentiments have large support in the Negro community. In one New England city, Dr. Darity found that 88 percent of the black males under 30 were opposed to abortion and almost half of them felt that encouragement of the use of birth control methods "is comparable to trying to eliminate [blacks] from society."

Additionally, some black nationalists have argued that it is important for the black population of this country to grow more rapidly than the white population so that Negroes can gain increasingly more political power. "The more people, the more power," they proclaim.

In the case of non-white citizens, the great majority of whom are Negroes, there is a wealth of population and birth data, particularly from a special Census Bureau study released last month.

The statisticians report that this country's black population is actually growing rapidly, both absolutely and relative to whites. Between 1950 and 1970 the number of Negroes in this country increased by 50 percent, from 15 million to 22.7 million persons, while the white population increased by less than one-third.

Two factors explain the difference in growth. One is the higher birth rate for non-whites. Over most of the past 20 years the non-white birth rate in this country has usually been 40 to 50 percent higher than the white birth rate. This marked difference has persisted even over the past decade when the birth rates of both groups have declined appreciably.

The second factor is the rapid decline in the non-white death rate since 1950. Over the past 20 years that rate has fallen about 15 percent, and has reached roughly the same level as the white death rate which has remained almost constant. Last December, in fact, the non-white death rate was slightly below the white death rate.

One significant result of these trends is the increased percentage of non-whites among the nation's youngest citizens. For the country as a whole, one person out of eight is non-white, but among Americans under five, about one child in six is now non-white. By census definition, it is worth noting, the "white" category includes Americans of Spanish origin — primarily Puerto Ricans and Mexican Americans — whose social, economic and demographic characteristics resemble those of blacks more closely than those of the descendants of European immigrants. Aside from Negroes, the "non-white" category includes Indians, Chinese, Japanese and Hawaiians.

A census calculation published two years ago suggests that if recent trends continue they could produce further appreciable changes in the "mix" of the American population. Census statisticians calculated what they call the "intrinsic rate of natural increase." This is an attempt to make white and non-white rates of population growth fully comparable by allowing for the differences in the age patterns of mothers and in the age patterns of deaths.

On this corrected basis, if 1967 trends were to continue for a substantial period of time, the white population would grow on the average by 5.6 persons per 1,000 women annually and the non-white population by 18.2 persons per 1000 women annually, or three times as rapidly.

Such calculations are pure exercises in theory, of course, for trends can and do change. Thus some statisticians argue that as non-whites rise in the economic scale and become better educated, their birth rates tend to fall in the same manner that birth rates of whites have declined. Demographers have stubbed their toes so often with predictions that have turned out to be wrong that they are reluctant now to make rigid forecasts for the future even as regards total American population growth, let alone its components.

Obituary: Motherhood

OPINION | BY ELLEN PECK | MAY 13, 1972

> OBITUARY: MOTHERHOOD. *Died, as a symbol, a life role, a sacred institution, sometime in the early nineteen-seventies. Causes of death: concern for overpopulation; and the desire of many to live as free individuals, not nurturers of young.*

Motherhood is losing ground.

Small signs of un-enshrinement are beginning to appear. At Mills College in California, the young valedictorian declares, "The best thing I can do for mankind is never to have children." In the ladies' lounge at La Guardia Airport, a woman juggling three infants is treated to a lecture on the population explosion. In Washington, D.C., an obstetrician routinely asks each patient who has missed a period, "Do you wish to terminate this pregnancy?" And a Midwestern epidemiologist believes that pregnancy today represents pathology, and not a state of health.

I suppose that I am part of this movement. My husband and I do not want children. We are tired of the polite slogans, the halfway, too-late measures sponsored by Planned Parenthood and Zero Population Growth. If "Planned Parenthood Is an Act of Love," planned non-parenthood is more so, since it shields more might-be-borns from an uncertain future.

Is "Stop at Two" a message which will stop our population growth? Not very soon (unless it is assumed that parents die soon after giving birth). Otherwise, within the 18-to-35-year age group, there is a population doubling; and as the children grow, requiring schools and cars and housing, the bulldozers move. And we are sick of being brutalized by bulldozers.

Once, there were good and valid reasons to have children. Once, it was inevitable. Once, there was nothing else to do. Once, human survival depended on human fertility. Once, the attainment of adulthood was marked by a desire to share one's values and delights in life with one's own children.

But these things are no longer true. Today, contraception and sterilization can be chosen; there is a world outside the home for women; our survival now rests with our ability to stop smothering the eco-system with our numbers; and parenthood, today, seems to us the very opposite of adulthood.

Many marriages do not survive the strains of parenthood; the birth of children too often means the dissolution of romance, the loss of freedom, the abandonment of ideals to economics.

Try weighing ideals against the $23,800 it costs (minimum) to raise one child to age eighteen. Watch a radical become a liberal (and a liberal a conservative) once the high cost of private schools is pondered.

Writer R. H. Gardner asked a poignant question once. "How many young men's dreams," he wondered, "have been sacrificed to the need for separate bedrooms for the children, an education at the college of their choice?" How many? Would anybody like to count?

A woman's ideals and her involvement with the larger world of the community can suffer, too. With 100 car pools every year, she simply has less time to care about the problems of the inner city. She knows there is wider world outside, but she must teach the alphabet, direct the play group. The talents and energies of too many of our women are largely lost to the strictures and routines of motherhood.

Though our birth rate is falling, our real numbers rise inexorably as, once every six seconds, a new American is born. Surely, it is time to change all this. There isn't any longer frontier out there. Our economy now needs fewer, not more, people. Immortality rests within a life itself, not in genetic copies; parenthood is no prerequisite to power or to life.

Surely it is wrong to think that we should all be parents. Indeed, given the complexities of the task and the urgent need to further curb our birth rate, it would be far wiser to regard parenthood as a specialized occupation — and childlessness as our cultural norm.

Who shall decide which couples are truly qualified for parenthood? (Let us hope there will be no committees.) In a free society, this choice must lie with individuals.

The frightening drain on our economic and environmental resources is well-documented. If we are to survive, non-parenthood must truly become an option that society in general accepts, respects, and — yes — encourages.

Mother's Day is over.

ELLEN PECK, a columnist, is author of "The Baby Trap."

Pill Use Rivaled by Sterilization, Survey Indicates

BY JANE E. BRODY | JULY 22, 1977

STERILIZATION NOW RIVALS the birth control pill as the leading contraceptive method used by married couples, according to the finding of a newly reported national survey.

The data, based on a sample of 3,403 persons and gathered in 1975, indicate that approximately 6.8 million married couples of childbearing age had chosen contraceptive sterilization (and an additional 1.1 million were sterilized for medical reasons), as against 7.1 million couples who were using the pill to prevent unwanted births.

The survey indicated that while the proportion of married women using the pill reached a plateau in recent years, contraceptive sterilization has grown tremendously in popularity since 1970. The increase in the proportion of sterilized couples was found to be greatest among those married 10 or more years. But even among couples married just five to nine years, 22 percent had chosen sterilization by 1975, compared with only 8 percent in 1970.

RATE INCREASING FOR WOMEN

The percentage of married couples in which either the husband or wife was sterilized for contraceptive reasons increased from 8.8 in 1965 to 16 in 1970 to 31.3 in 1975. Among older couples, those married 20 to 24 years, the use of sterilization increased from 37 percent of couples to 55.7 percent in the two years from 1973 to 1975.

Among couples who have had all the children they want, 43.5 percent had been sterilized by 1975 as against 24.1 percent using the pill for contraception.

Since 1973, the survey indicated, female sterilization has been increasing somewhat more rapidly than male sterilization, but thus far the proportion of couples in which the wife has been sterilized, 16.3

percent, is not much different from the proportion in which the husband has been sterilized, 15 percent.

Overall, the survey found, the proportion of married couples using the most effective methods of birth control increased dramatically in the decade since 1965. In that year, 38 percent of a national sample of married couples were using either the pill, the intrauterine device (I.U.D.) or sterilization for contraception. By 1975, an estimated 75 percent of married couples were using one of these methods.

The details behind this "extraordinary development" in contraceptive practices are described by Dr. Charles F. Westoff and Elise F. Jones in the July-August issue of Family Planning Perspectives, the scientific journal of the Planned Parenthood Federation of America. Dr. Westoff is director of the Office of Population Research at Princeton University, where Elise Jones is a research associate.

The survey is the fourth in a series of National Fertility Studies directed by Drs. Westoff and Norman B. Ryder, also a population researcher at Princeton. The surveys are financed by the National Institute of Child Health and Human Development, a division of the National Institutes of Health in Bethesda, Md.

The 1975 survey, for purposes of accurate statistical analysis of trends, was restricted to a sample of 3,403 white women below age 45 who were married only once to men who were also married only once.

By comparing the new data with the results of the previous fertility studies in 1965, 1970 and 1973, the researchers were able to derive an estimate of the contraceptive practices of all currently married women of reproductive age in the United States.

The number of blacks in each category would have been too small for accurate statistical analysis in the 1975 survey, which primarily involved reinterviewing women who had been interviewed initially in 1970. Instead, the researchers made an extrapolation from the findings of the previous fertility studies, assuming that the same kinds of changes had taken place among the groups not included in the 1975 survey as among those interviewed.

They concluded that although "the pill remains the most popular method of birth control among women married fewer than 10 years, surgical sterilization is now the most commonly used method of birth control among couples married 10 years or more, as well as among couples who have had all the children they intend" to have.

Use of the pill has been stable since 1970 among married women in general, but has declined substantially since 1973 among women married 15 years or more, the survey indicated. In 1975 34 percent of continuously married women used the pill. In the same year, among 31 percent of the couples, either the husband or wife had undergone a contraceptive sterilization operation, nearly double the percentage of sterilized couples in 1970.

At the same time, the use of the I.U.D., which had increased sharply between 1965 and 1973 — from 1.1 percent to 9.5 percent of married couples — dropped slightly to 8.7 percent by 1975. The authors suggested that the highly publicized hazards of the Dalkon shield, a type of intrauterine device, and its subsequent withdrawal from the market may have frightened some women away from I.U.D.'s in general.

The researchers found no support for the widespread belief that the diaphragm was making a comeback. Use of the diaphragm continued to decline from 10.5 percent in 1965 to 5.7 percent in 1970 to 3.9 percent in 1975. The authors said it was possible that more young women were now using the diaphragm to space their pregnancies, but that in any case the percentage of such users remained very small.

Similarly, use of the condom dropped by half, from 22 percent of couples in 1965 to 10.9 percent in 1975, although in recent years its use has risen slightly among couples married fewer than 10 years.

Planned Parenthood's New Head Takes a Fighting Stand

BY JUDY KLEMESRUD | FEB. 3, 1978

FAYE WATTLETON, the new president designate of the Planned Parenthood Federation of America, said in New York yesterday that she was "putting the world on notice" that the traditionally lowkeyed organization was going to become more aggressive in the battle for abortion rights.

Miss Wattleton, who is the first woman, the first black and the youngest (34 years old) president in Planned Parenthood's history, said that the new aggressive stance was necessary to combat the burgeoning activities and successes of the family planning organization's "enemies" — anti-abortion members of the so-called "right-to-life" movement.

"What has happened is that we've allowed them to have center stage," she said at a press conference held to announce her selection at Planned Parenthood's headquarters, 810 Seventh Avenue. "I'd like to say those days are over."

Miss Wattleton, currently a Planned Parenthood official in Dayton, Ohio, who is married and has one child, added: "Many of us had become complacent because of our victories in the 1960's and early 1970's. There was a feeling among many of us that right would win out. But so many events of the past year, especially the Federal and state actions limiting payments for abortion under Medicaid, have made us realize that we must become more aggressive."

Miss Wattleton said that during her three-year, $70,000-a-year term, she would have three principal public policy targets:

- "To restore to the poor access to safe, legal abortions so cruelly destroyed in two-thirds of the states by recent Federal and state actions limiting payments for abortion under Medicaid."

- "To place reproductive biology research and contraceptive development at the highest level on the nation's research agenda."

- "To formulate and pursue a national strategy for reducing the incidence of teenage pregnancy."

"Pregnancy rates among sexually active adolescents were as high in 1976 as they were in 1971," she read angrily from a statement. "Only one out of seven pregnant girls used contraception, and eight out of ten teenage pregnancies were unintended. Much needs to be done in health services and educational programs if the tragic prospect of many hundreds of thousands of children bearing children each year is to be ended."

'WATCHDOG POSITION'

When asked in an interview whether her being black would help diffuse criticism from some black groups that birth control and abortion are forms of black genocide, Miss Wattleton replied:

"I don't think a lot of people are yelling genocide anymore. Because I am black, I'm in a watchdog position on these issues, and no one should assume I've been co-opted. What better way is there to guard against those types of abuses?"

She added that when it came to the advancement of blacks, "we should not be concerned with increasing our numbers, but with the quality of life. What's really important is that black women have equal access to determining when and how they will have children."

On another controversial issue, sterilization abuse, Miss Wattleton said she endorsed proposed Federal guidelines that would require, among other things, a 30-day waiting period before a person could become sterilized, to avoid possible coercion. Some opponents of the guidelines argue that sterilization should be available on demand, with no restrictions.

"We think the one-month waiting period is reasonable," Miss Wattleton said. "But we are also concerned that the pendulum doesn't swing too far in the other direction, so that it limits access to sterilization. People have the right to decide to be sterilized, just as the affluent do, and with abortion restrictions, more and more women are going to want sterilization."

IN CHARGE OF HEADQUARTERS

Miss Wattleton was selected for the presidency on Jan. 27, "after a search that took exactly nine months," she said with a smile, at a meeting of Planned Parenthood's national board of directors in Kansas City. As president, she will be in charge of the headquarters staff in New York and 189 community-based affiliates in 43 states and the District of Columbia. Last year, those affiliates provided family planning services to more than 1.1 million persons.

Planned Parenthood, which has a budget of $90 million, employs 3,000 staff members nationwide and utilizes more than 20,000 volunteers.

Miss Wattleton's new job will pit her head-to-head with another articulate black woman — Dr. Mildred Jefferson, a Boston surgeon who heads the National Right-to-Life Movement. But Miss Wattleton doesn't think that their similarities had anything to do with her selection.

"I thought about it a lot," she conceded, "and I think I was chosen for my knowledge of the organization, and for being a woman, and because we needed to change our image — not because we wanted to emulate our enemies."

Miss Wattleton was born in St. Louis, the only child of the late George Wattleton, who worked in a trunk factory, and his wife, Ozie, a housewife. She worked her way through Ohio State University, where she earned a degree in nursing, and then went on to Columbia University where she received her master's degree in nursing.

It was while she was at Columbia during 1966-67 that she first became interested in family planning, she said. "The majority of my clinical experience was spent at Harlem Hospital, and one day I saw a 17-year-old girl die from a botched abortion. That had a greater impact on me than anything else I saw."

JOHN SOTO/THE NEW YORK TIMES

"Many of us had become complacent," said Faye Wattleton, "because of our victories in the 1960's and early 1970's."

Miss Wattleton, who is 5 feet 11 inches tall, slender, and once worked as a fashion model, is currently executive director of Planned Parenthood of the Miami Valley (Dayton, Ohio). She and her husband, Franklin Gordon, mental health administrator, will move to New York in mid-April when Miss Wattleton assumes the Planned Parenthood presidency.

Their daughter, Felicia, is 2 years old. "She was very planned," Miss Wattleton said yesterday, with a smile.

CHAPTER 5

New Technologies

Throughout the 1980s and the 1990s, birth control became much more accepted in the United States. This was due, largely, to new technological developments and new birth control methods on the market. During these two decades, birth control pills with lower doses of hormones and fewer side effects were developed, as well as a copper intrauterine device (IUD), known as ParaGard. The first contraceptive implant, called Norplant, and an injectable birth control, known as Depo-Provera, were also released during this time.

Injected Contraceptive: Hazard or Boon?

BY PHILIP M. BOFFEY | JAN. 11, 1983

WASHINGTON, JAN. 10 — A rare public board of inquiry opened a five-day hearing today to evaluate whether the drug Depo-Provera is an almost ideal contraceptive for women — or a potential cause of cancer, birth defects and other disease.

The drug is already used in more than 80 countries and is enthusiastically endorsed by population control groups because a single injection prevents ovulation and conception for at least three months.

Dr. Elizabeth B. Connell, professor of gynecology and obstetrics at the Emory University School of Medicine in Atlanta, told the board today that she had polled 20 experts and found that they ranked Depo-Provera ahead of all other contraceptives, including the pill, intrauterine devices, the condom and diaphragm. At a news conference held earlier, she said that Depo-Provera "comes very very close to the ideal" contraceptive.

The drug's chief virtues, according to its adherents, are that it is highly effective, remains effective even if the user is a few weeks late in obtaining a repeat injection, and requires less motivation than the pill, which must be taken daily, or barrier contraceptives, which must be applied at the time of intercourse. The drug can be administered by any person who normally gives injections in a health care system.

"Depo-Provera is the most effective method of reversible contraception available today," Dr. Daniel R. Mishell Jr., chairman of obstetrics and gynecology at the University of Southern California School of Medicine, testified today. Both he and Dr. Connell appeared on behalf of the drug's manufacturer, the Upjohn Company, which is seeking permission to market the drug for contraceptive use in this country.

But Depo-Provera must clear a major hurdle if it is to be approved for marketing: It has produced cancers in both strains of animals given long-term exposure in the tests required by the Food and Drug Administration. It produced breast cancers when administered to beagle dogs for seven years and, just to show that was no fluke, it produced them again in a followup beagle study. And it produced cancers of the endometrium (lining of the uterus) when administered to monkeys in high doses for 10 years.

Questions have also been raised as to whether the drug is apt to cause birth defects in fetuses that are inadvertently exposed to it, either because the contraceptive fails or a woman is unwittingly pregnant at the time she receives the injection.

Critics contend that if the drug starts to cause harm in a woman or fetus, its long-lasting action is no longer a virtue but rather a vice — there is no way to purge the drug from the bloodstream.

Based on an extensive analysis of the data then available, the Food and Drug Administration in 1978 refused to approve the drug for contraceptive use in this country. The agency said that safe and better-studied contraceptives were already on the market and that it could identify no significant group of American patients for whom the benefits of Depo-Provera would outweigh the risks. On Tuesday the agency will field an array of Government and academic scientists to reiterate that position, taking into account four more years of data.

'A CLOSE CALL'

One of witnesses who will testify Tuesday, Robert J. Temple, acting director of the F.D.A.'s Office of New Drug Evaluation, acknowledged in remarks submitted for the record that the decision was "not an open and shut case" and had been considered "a close call, a hard decision by everyone in the agency who has looked at the question." But he said tumors found in animals are "alarming enough for us to think that it shouldn't be approved — that's the main basis for concluding that the drug is not safe."

The dispute reflects a fundamental difference of opinion among scientists over how much weight to put on the animal tests as opposed to human experience. The drug's supporters say animal results in this case are not relevant to humans and that millions of women throughout the world have used the drug safely. But the drug's critics treat the animal results as a warning of danger and put little stock in limited human studies that show no adverse effects.

The drug is supported by a glittering array of health and population groups, including the World Health Organization, the American College of Obstetrics and Gynecology, the International Planned Parenthood Federation and the Population Crisis Committee. Two women who are officials of the Population Crisis Committee have been telling reporters that they are part of a "growing underground" of Depo-Provera users in this country who find it a safe and highly effective contraceptive. The drug has also been endorsed by an expert advisory committee to the Agency for International Development and, for at least limited use, by two F.D.A. advisory panels.

The chief opponents of the drug are F.D.A. staff scientists, individual scientists from the National Cancer Institute, the national Centers for Disease Control, the Environmental Protection Agency, a few academic experts and health writers, the National Women's Health Network and Ralph Nader's Health Research Group, which played a key role in blocking approval of the drug in 1978.

Upjohn, the drug's manufacturer, estimates that up to four million American women might switch from other contraceptives to Depo-Provera if the F.D.A. approves it for contraceptive purposes in this country.

Depo-Provera or drugs very much like it have been used for decades to treat a variety of ailments. Their contraceptive action was discovered somewhat by accident in the mid-1960's. The current product consists of an active ingredient, a drug known as depotmedroxyprogesterone acetate, suspended in tiny crystals in a watery solution. It is typically injected into the muscle of the upper arm or buttock, and it is released slowly into the bloodstream from the injection site.

The drug exerts its contraceptive effect chiefly by preventing ovulation; it acts upon the hypothalamus and pituitary gland to suppress two hormones that would otherwise bring about the maturation and release of an egg. Several secondary effects — notably changes in the cervical mucus, uterine lining, and Fallopian tubes — also help reduce fertility.

Depo-Provera contains only a progestogen and not the estrogens that are responsible for many of the side effects of most oral contraceptives. It does, however, cause menstrual bleeding in some women and stoppage of bleeding in others. There is also a delay in return to fertility among women who discontinue the drug so as to become pregnant. And some users have complained of loss of libido, weight gain and mood changes, among other side effects.

The chief focus of the hearings will be the validity of the animal and human studies. Upjohn witnesses argued today that the beagle was not an appropriate model for judging the effect of the drug in humans because beagles can develop breast tumors from progestens alone, whereas humans and other animals apparently require that other hormones be present at the same time. The World Health Organization and at least three medical review committees have also concluded that the beagle is not an appropriate model for evaluating the risk of breast cancer in humans.

Upjohn witnesses also contended that the endometrial cancers found in two monkeys given 50 times the human contraceptive dose could have been spontaneous or could have arisen from plaque-forming cells that are not present in women. At any rate, Upjohn said, the number of cancers is too small to draw firm conclusions.

SEEN AS CAUSE FOR CONCERN

But Government scientists plan to argue Tuesday that, even if the dogs and monkeys do not exactly mimic the effects in humans, the findings are cause for concern. In advance testimony, Dr. Renate Kimbrough, of the Centers for Disease Control, contends that a substance that causes cancer in animal tissue not present in humans may well cause cancer in some entirely different human organs. She also suggests that humans may conceivably be more susceptible to carcinogenic effects from Depo-Provera than the animals were.

Upjohn witnesses argued today that the "theoretical concerns about an increased risk of cancer" in humans have not materialized in clinical studies or epidemiologic surveys or voluntary reporting systems around the world, even though 100,000 women have used the drug for a decade or more and two million now use it.

But Dr. Robert N. Hoover, acting chief of environmental epidemiology at the National Cancer Institute, plans to argue that existing epidemiologic studies are inadequate because of poor design, small numbers, lack of control groups, sampling bias, too brief a period of followup or limited exposures of subjects to the drug.

After weighing the conflicting evidence, the board of inquiry will make a recommendation to the Commissioner of Food and Drugs, Arthur Hull Hayes Jr., who must make the final decision on Upjohn's application.

Courts Block Federal Rule on Contraceptives

BY MARGOT SLADE AND WAYNE BIDDLE | FEB. 20, 1983

THE REAGAN ADMINISTRATION'S stated goal of fostering closer ties between parent and child may have been well-meant, but two Federal courts last week said the means — regulations requiring federally funded clinics to notify parents if teen-agers receive contraceptives — were unlawful.

"As a result of the regulations, substantial numbers of adolescents will become pregnant and will either elect abortion or suffer the consequences of unwanted pregnancies," said Judge Thomas A. Flannery in Washington, D.C. And that, said Judge Henry F. Werker in New York, separately making the same point, "constitutes a blatant disregard" for one of Congress's main purposes in providing Federal funds to combat the problems of teen-age pregnancy.

Each court issued preliminary injunctions preventing the regulations from taking effect on schedule this Friday in more than 4,100 clinics nationwide. The Administration last week said it would appeal the New York ruling; there was no decision on an appeal of the Washington case.

At issue is how to carry out the intent of Congress to stem the number of adolescent pregnancies while at the same time "encouraging family participation" in a youngster's decision concerning contraceptives. About 450,000 girls under age 18 become pregnant each year.

There is also a question of what Congress meant by "encourage." Most clinics say they fulfill that requirement by trying to persuade teen-age clients to talk with their parents about contraceptive use.

Last year, however, the Reagan Administration said that "encourage" meant clinics themselves must notify parents or guardians within 10 days of giving teen-agers under age 18 prescription contraceptives. Exceptions would be granted only in cases where the teen-ager might suffer physical harm. Without this notification, said Richard S. Schweiker, then Secretary of Health and Human Services, parents would not have a chance to participate. Mr. Schweiker said parental notification did not mandate family involvement but facilitated it.

Judge Werker called the argument "sophistry," accepting instead statistical and medical documentation submitted by the New York State Department of Health that "parental notification would deter adolescents from obtaining prescription contraceptives."

Recent studies support the notion that many teen-agers will forgo contraception — but not sex — rather than let their parents know they are sexually active. In 1979 and 1980, the Alan Guttmacher Institute, a research organization financed by Planned Parenthood Federation of America, surveyed 1,200 unmarried minors receiving contraceptives at 53 family-planning clinics across the country. About 24 percent said they would stop using birth control methods if parental notification were mandated. A recent study of 1,200 teen-agers in eight cities, conducted by Johns Hopkins University, found confidentiality the most important consideration in the choice of a clinic.

Why a Lag in Male-Oriented Birth Control?

BY JANE E. BRODY | OCT. 16, 1983

THOUGH SCIENCE'S UNDERSTANDING of male reproductive physiology has leapfrogged in the last decade, the research has not yet produced effective, easy-to-use contraceptives for men. Only one method, the century-old condom, is both as effective and safe as some of the contraceptives available to women.

The outlook for male contraceptives is not much brighter. A report by The Alan Guttmacher Institute, issued just over a week ago, outlined 11 new birth control techniques "on the horizon"; only two were for men. Even those — gossypol, a cottonseed oil derivative that interferes with sperm production, and synthetic forms of the brain hormone LHRH, which turns off testicular function, have at least eight years of experimentation and testing before they are commercially viable, assuming their serious side effects can be circumvented. The World Health Organization has said it might be more than 20 years before a new male contraceptive is marketable.

That leaves men with very few alternatives: withdrawal, a technique that effectively suppressed population growth in France and other European countries until about 1960; the condom, and vasectomy. Women can choose from among 11 contraceptives.

Many feminists believe male chauvinism led to this inequality. Many experts agree it has been a major factor, though not the only one. Women themselves bear some responsibility. Margaret Sanger and other leaders of the American birth control movement in the early 1900's wanted to give women control of their own fertility; they ignored male contraception. Through the years, advocates of birth control have continued emphasizing female contraception. Moreover, men perform the bulk of contraceptive research and some people believe that male researchers feel more comfortable tampering with a woman's physiology than with their own.

Dr. Wayne Bardin, director of biomedical research at the Population Council in New York, says medicine has reinforced the focus on female contraception. There has long been an established medical specialty in obstetrics and gynecology, but no comparable specialty devoted to the male reproductive system. Urologists, whose province it could be, concentrate on genitourinary abnormalities. The few who specialize in reproductive problems are concerned with male infertility.

Behind the sexual politics and proclivities of the medical profession, however, basic biology remains the greatest barrier to developing male contraceptives.

A woman produces only one fertile egg a month. A man produces perhaps 30 million sperm a day, any one of which can impregnate an egg. In plain terms, it is simpler to disrupt production of one egg than millions of sperm, particularly since a drug that reduces sperm production 90 percent might still leave a man fertile. It may also be safer for the fetus. A woman is born with a lifetime supply of eggs. But a man's sperm form daily and can be genetically damaged during that formative process by, say, sperm-blocking chemicals.

OPPORTUNITIES TO INTERVENE

The organ that produces sperm also makes the male sex hormone testosterone, which is responsible for libido, potency and secondary sex characteristics, such as a deep voice. Medical experts have found that shutting down sperm production also shuts down testosterone, resulting in impotence and loss of libido. (Experimental contraceptives have their own side effects, including shrinking of the testicles, breast enlargement and increases in blood cholesterol.) By contrast, ovarian function need not be wholly suppressed to prevent ovulation. And since a woman's libido is not a function of ovarian hormones, but of other sex hormones produced in the adrenal glands, side effects are more easily avoided.

The process of conception can be disrupted at various points: the release of the egg, the migration of sperm to the egg, fertilization, the implantation of the fertilized egg in the uterine wall. Male fertility can be interrupted only at the site of sperm production, maturation or release, and even these sites can prove unworkable. Since it takes sperm about three months to develop to the point of release, a drug that suppresses the production process would not become fully effective for three to six months. A return to fertility would be similarly delayed.

Whereas synthetic hormones that control female fertility are effective orally, those that stop sperm production are inactivated in the digestive tract. According to Dr. Gabriel Bialy, director of contraceptive development at the National Institute of Child Health and Human Development, R & D in male contraceptives has thus centered on drugs that can be implanted under the skin, administered through injection or, perhaps, inhaled.

The institute is spending about twice as much on developing contraceptives for women as for men. The Population Council has allocated its money in a similar fashion. Dr. S. Bruce Schearer of the Population Resource Center in New York says the major drug companies are researching male contraception, but admits the focus is on women. "This is because none of the male methods is far along," Dr. Bardin said. "Nothing we've tried has made it to the final phase of clinical testing."

The Perfect Contraceptive: When?

EDITORIAL | BY THE NEW YORK TIMES | JULY 1, 1985

NOW THAT THOUSANDS of American drugstores maintain a "family-planning center," it's hard to believe that state laws forbidding birth control by married couples were struck down only 20 years ago. Americans now assume that contraceptives are available to all. They are wrong.

More than three million American women experience unintended pregnancies each year. Only 41 percent of the world's married couples of reproductive age use modern means of contraception. For some of those who don't, contraception is undesirable. For countless others it is unavailable or unsafe.

No available contraceptive is ideal, and some of the more effective ones, like the pill and the I.U.D., are apt to produce side effects. The condom is culturally rejected in many places. Sterilization is highly effective but usually irreversible. All else failing, more than 40 million women a year resort to abortion, which is surely not contraception.

What's needed, then, are contraceptives that are safe, effective, easy to use and inexpensive and better methods of counseling about their use. Nor should they be only for women. The prototype for the modern condom appeared in the 16th century. Surely it's more than time for the development of a new male contraceptive.

Will they be available anytime soon? Not nearly soon enough to prevent millions of unintended pregnancies, large numbers of them ending in maternal death or abortion. The world spent only $175 million for research in the field last year, most of it for reproductive biology rather than contraceptive development.

Some experts think it would take at least $500 million a year over several decades to exploit promising new leads in long-acting, anti-fertility vaccines and reversible nonsurgical methods of sterilization. Such research isn't possible in the third world, which is where it's needed most; therefore the burden falls on the West — on American and international agencies, foundations and pharmaceutical companies. Should their investment succeed, the return would be extraordinary: They would have done the world a favor.

Contraceptives' Presence in Schools Creates a Dispute Among Educators

BY JANE PERLEZ | OCT. 13, 1986

AT NINE NEW YORK CITY high schools over the past two years, state-financed health clinics have provided health care to low-income students, including birth-control counseling.

Clinics at two of the schools dispensed contraceptive devices to students who had parental permission to use the health services; at the other seven schools, prescriptions for contraceptives were written and the students were referred to the affiliated hospitals and clinics to have them filled.

The health clinics, run by major hospitals or community health centers, were approved by the Board of Education in 1984. But at the time, members were not informed that the dispensing of birth-control devices and prescriptions would be among the services.

The availability of contraceptives, revealed in a report to the board 10 days ago, came as a surprise to board members with the exception of the president, Robert F. Wagner Jr., who said he had learned of it earlier.

To Mr. Wagner, Schools Chancellor Nathan Quinones and Mayor Koch, the prescriptions and dispensing of birth-control devices was not a shock. "Anyone who believes comprehensive health care for sexually active adolescents does not include birth control is crazy," Mr. Wagner said.

There was considerable disagreement among the seven board members. Two said they opposed both prescription writing and distribution of contraceptives. Two others indicated they were opposed to distribution. Only three, including Mr. Wagner, fully supported the policy.

One board member, Dr. Gwendolyn C. Baker, said she believed the distribution of contraceptives encouraged promiscuity, a view that was echoed by the Roman Catholic Archdiocese of New York City and the Diocese of Brooklyn.

THE BACKGROUND

In an effort to stem the rise of teen-age pregnancies around the nation, health clinics that provide family planning counseling have been rapidly increasing in public schools.

The Center for Population Options, a private nonprofit group based in Washington that seeks to prevent unwanted teen-age pregnancies, says the number of school-based health clinics has grown from 12 in 1980 to 61 today. At least 10 clinics, the center said, dispensed contraceptives at the school clinic, and about 40 more have physicians who write prescriptions for the devices.

In New York City, girls as young as 11 and 12 who attend junior high schools are becoming pregnant, according to Mr. Quinones. In 1984, 14,431 girls age 17 or younger became pregnant in New York City. There were 1,259 pregnancies among girls under 15.

A report this year by researchers at the Johns Hopkins School of Medicine showed that counseling and birth-control services to students at two health clinics at public schools in Baltimore delayed sexual activity and decreased pregnancies.

With these statistics and the general need for student health services in mind, the New York State Department of Health made $1.5 million available for establishment of the nine school health clinics in New York City. Chosen by the hospitals in consultation with the schools, the nine schools have heavy populations of low-income students, many of whom have never seen a family doctor, said Alice Radosh, the coordinator of Adolescent Pregnancy and Parenting Services in the Mayor's office.

The nine schools and their health providers are: Andrew Jackson in Queens (Jamaica Hospital); William H. Taft in the Bronx (Bronx Lebanon Hospital); Boys and Girls in Brooklyn (Bedford-Stuyvesant Family Health Center); Louis D. Brandeis and Martin Luther King Jr.,

(St. Luke's Hospital); Manhattan Center for Mathematics and Science, and Julia Richman (Mount Sinai Medical Center), and West Side and Park East (Ryan Community Health Center) in Manhattan.

FOR CONTRACEPTIVES

Mayor Koch, the United Federation of Teachers, the New York City Council of Churches, an array of children's advocacy groups, as well as Mr. Quinones and Mr. Wagner, vigorously support dispensing of birth-control devices at school clinics, although most add the caveat that parental permission should be obtained.

Mr. Wagner said he believed contraceptives should be distributed in the school health clinics. By dispensing contraceptives, he said, the health clinics were not doing anything that hospitals and community health clinics were already doing without parental consent.

Ms. Radosh dismissed a suggestion by Dr. Baker, the only black member of the board, that the clinics were selectively placed in schools with high numbers of black and Hispanic students. Ms. Radosh said that national studies showed that teen-agers who were poor and not doing well in school were most likely to become pregnant. More black and Hispanic students in New York City — who make up 75 percent of the student population — come from poor backgrounds than white students, Ms. Radosh said.

AGAINST CONTRACEPTIVES

Two members of the Board of Education, Dr. Baker and Dr. Stephen R. Franse, were opposed to the prescription-writing and the distribution of birth-control devices. Dr. Irene Impellizzeri, another board member, opposed the dispensing of contraceptives on a variety of grounds, but supported the writing of prescriptions within the "privileged relationship" between doctor and patient. A fourth board member, James F. Regan, could not be reached during the week but board officials said he was understood to be opposed to the dispensing of contraceptives, not the writing of prescriptions.

Dr. Baker, who is the executive director of the national Young Women's Christian Association, said she believed dispensing contraceptives encouraged promiscuity among teen-agers. Further, she said, the policy opened the door to further involvement in the sexual lives of students. In another 10 years, sterilization might be suggested, she said.

Of greatest importance, Dr. Baker said, was the role of the school to "build character" and develop a "value system" for students so that sex would be less dominant in their lives.

THE OUTLOOK

A vigorous discussion of the school health clinics is expected at a Board of Education meeting Wednesday. The school board is expected to allow the clinics to continue to exist and expand to other schools. Mr. Wagner has repeatedly stated he wants four more health clinics to open in junior high schools. But Mr. Wagner has made it clear the four proposed junior high school clinics would deal only with physical examinations and treatment of illnesses, and would not dispense either contraceptives or prescriptions for them.

In addition, Mr. Wagner said he would ask for a modification. Only students 18 years old and over would be given birth-control devices, he said. Students under 18, with parental consent to use the health clinics, could have contraceptive prescriptions only.

Cash-for-Sterilization Plan Draws Addicts and Critics

BY PAM BELLUCK | JULY 24, 1999

THE BILLBOARDS MAKE an unusual offer.

"If you are addicted to drugs," they say, "get birth control — get $200 cash."

The signs, which went up recently in neighborhoods in Chicago, advertise a program that will start in New York on Monday, intended to persuade drug-addicted women to get sterilized or get long-term birth control like Norplant or Depo-Privera. Once the women offer proof of that, they will be given $200 in cash.

Called Crack, for Children Requiring a Caring Kommunity, the privately financed campaign is an offshoot of one that began in California about 18 months ago and appears to be catching on. Billboards have gone up in Florida and Minnesota. And women in Pennsylvania, New Hampshire and Michigan have already received money after taking the required steps, according to the group's Web site, www.cracksterilization.com.

The Chicago offshoot, which is also distributing fliers at health clinics, is the first to open other than the program's headquarters in Anaheim. It will be run by a social worker.

The program has attracted considerable attention. Groups including Planned Parenthood and the American Civil Liberties Union say the tactics coerce poor women whose judgment is clouded by drugs into doing something they may regret.

"It's simply a bribe for sterilization, and that's improper and it's wrong," said Steve Trombley, the president and chief executive officer of Planned Parenthood of Chicago.

The program was started by a California woman, Barbara Harris, after she adopted four children from the same drug-addicted mother.

"I thought, 'Here's this irresponsible woman walking around having babies yearly and she can do that just because she has a right to get pregnant,' " Ms. Harris said in an interview today. "She has no intention of raising them."

Ms. Harris tried, unsuccessfully, to get state legislation passed that would "make it a crime to have a drug-addicted baby," she said. Then she took matters into her own hands and decided to start paying for sterilization and birth control.

While it is an unorthodox method, the Crack program reflects broader efforts by states in recent years to penalize women who behave in ways that could harm their unborn children. Court cases in 21 states have sought to make it a crime for pregnant women to abuse alcohol or drugs. In 20 states, those prosecutions have failed, but in South Carolina in 1997, the State Supreme Court ruled that a pregnant crack addict was guilty under the state's child-abuse laws. A similar case in Wisconsin is working its way through the appellate system.

And three states, South Dakota, South Carolina and Wisconsin, passed fetal abuse laws last year, either mandating that substance-abusing pregnant women be forced into detoxification programs or subjecting them to jail time.

Ms. Harris says she is having no trouble getting private donations for her work, including one for $5,000 from Dr. Laura Schlessinger, the conservative radio talk show host.

So far, Ms. Harris said, her organization has paid 57 women who have been pregnant a total of 423 times. "They had 161 abortions and gave birth 262 times," she said. "Forty of those babies died and 175 are in foster care."

The women have to submit documents, like an arrest report, to show they are on drugs. And after they get the birth control procedures, usually paid for with government assistance, they send in written proof.

One woman to respond to the campaign was Sharon Adams, 38, a former crack addict from the South-Central section of Los Angeles.

Ms. Adams had 14 children and saw 4 of them die and 9 placed in foster care. Ms. Adams, who had a tubal ligation through the program, said she was free of drugs now and raising her youngest child. "I know I needed to get my tubes tied," Ms. Adams said, "but the $200 kind of motivated me."

A Chicago woman, Marlo Purnell, said today she planned to take advantage of the offer and get Norplant. Ms. Purnell, 31, said she was a crack addict who had had to give up custody of her five children, ages 14 months to 10 years. She said she would use the $200 to "probably pay some of my bills, like my phone bill," and that she hoped to have more children "once I get my life together."

Critics of the program say that its billboards target mostly minority neighborhoods. Ms. Harris, who is white and runs the program almost single-handedly, responds that she cannot be racist, since her husband, a surgical technician, is black and nearly half of the women she has paid are white.

A larger worry, critics say, is that women may feel coerced into giving up their ability to have children, and not get any help to stop using drugs.

Priscilla Smith, deputy director of litigation for the Center for Reproductive Law and Policy, said, "All you're doing is supporting their drug habit and you're taking away an important thing from them for when they may get healthy."

Proponents of the program say they are aware that the women may simply spend the money on drugs.

"I don't care what they do — as long as they get their tubes tied," said Frank Peard, a 70-year-old retiree who helped arrange for Crack billboards to be put up in Fort Pierce, Fla., and has contributed $400 to the cause. "As far as I'm concerned they could buy a gun and shoot themselves with it. That's the least of the evils. The evil is producing these children when they don't plan to take care of them."

Beyond Birth Control: The Pill Tackles New Duties

BY ANNETTE FUENTES | MAY 7, 2002

LORI RICE WAS 10 when she started menstruating, and every month was an ordeal. "I was having a lot of problems with my period — cramping and heavy bleeding," said Lori, now 15. "The pain was the worst. I missed a lot of school, and it got worse the longer I had my period."

Her mother, Kathy Rice, took Lori to their family doctor, who prescribed heat, ibuprofen and calcium supplements. Heat gave Lori some relief, but it was not always a practical or sufficient solution.

"One time I was in class and in so much pain, the teacher let me go lie down on the heater in the back of the classroom," she recalled.

Finally, Lori and her mother went to Dr. Gina Sucato, an assistant professor of pediatrics and a specialist in pediatric gynecology at the University of Pittsburgh. Dr. Sucato prescribed birth control pills to treat the dysmenorrhea, which encompasses symptoms including pain, nausea, vomiting and fainting. Lori has been on the pill for just a couple of months now, but she says she is like a new person. The blood flow is lighter and the pain has eased.

"I still have some cramping, but I can go to school," Lori said. "I used to be very mean that time of month. Now, my mood swings have changed. The only thing it hasn't done that it was supposed to is clear up my skin, but I hope it will."

Since 1960, when the Food and Drug Administration approved it for contraception, the pill has been one of the most effective methods of preventing pregnancy, and for adult women, it has been regularly prescribed to treat menstrual irregularities, dysmenorrhea and other gynecological conditions.

But in recent years, combined oral contraceptives — typically containing the hormones estrogen and progestin — have increasingly been prescribed for adolescent and teenage girls for noncontraceptive purposes. Several reasons drive this trend.

First, today's oral contraceptive is vastly different from the one that debuted 40 years ago. The early pill contained high doses of estrogen, and by 1962 was linked to blood clots and strokes. Now oral contraceptives are low-dose and considered safe for a vast majority of women of all ages.

Second, the F.D.A. approved oral contraceptives to treat acne in 1997 after clinical trials financed by the pill manufacturers proved them effective. Several oral contraceptives are marketed for acne.

Uses for oral contraceptives for adolescents have changed considerably from what they were five years ago, said Dr. Joseph Sanfilippo, the vice chairman of reproductive sciences at the University of Pittsburgh and the editor of The Journal of Pediatric and Adolescent Gynecology. "What comes to mind first is acne," Dr. Sanfilippo said. "I see the moms bringing in their daughters, who are now picking up on this use of the pill, not only from magazines, but from the Internet."

Treating acne or menstrual cramps may be the motivation for taking the pill, but there is a long list of additional benefits girls will experience, Dr. Sanfilippo said.

The pill lowers the risk of pelvic inflammatory disease, a common problem for teenagers, by improving the cervical mucus barrier against bacteria. It causes lighter menstrual flow and eliminates irregular bleeding, which can contribute to anemia, another problem for teenagers.

Oral contraceptives are also linked to reduced risk of ovarian, endometrial and uterine cancers.

"The story continues with bone-mineral density," said Dr. Sanfilippo. "We now know the objective is for a woman to enter menopause with maximum bone mineral density. So why not start as an adolescent? The estrogen facilitates maintaining bone-mineral density."

A majority of teenage girls who request the pill do so for birth control, Dr. Sanfilippo said. But relief from dysmenorrhea represents at least a significant number, with estimates of the percentage of teenagers suffering from some form of the condition ranging from 20 to 90, with 15 percent experiencing severe symptoms. At Columbia-Presbyterian Medical Center in New York, Dr. Anne R. Davis is conducting the first study of oral contraceptives in treating adolescents' menstrual pain.

"We're trying to get a sense of whether they miss less school and other activities," said Dr. Davis, an assistant professor of obstetrics and gynecology. "We're also looking at whether adolescents who are more depressed and have more stress and poor self-esteem have less benefit in terms of their pain treatment."

Still, Amy Allina, program director of the National Women's Health Network, a Washington policy group, says she is concerned that hormonal treatments, whose long-term effects on women are still unclear, are being pushed for the wrong reasons. No young woman should experience debilitating pain each month, Ms. Allina said, but she worries about what will happen down the road. While the research on low-dose estrogen is mostly positive, Ms. Allina said, girls and women still need to know the benefits and risks of hormonal contraception so that they can then make informed choices.

While adolescents seem to suffer from menstrual pain more than older women, it is not clear whether that is because dysmenorrhea eases over time or because adult women are better at dealing with it, Dr. Davis said. "Older women probably cope a little better," she said. "They know how to get hold of a medication, how to anticipate that it'll happen."

Over all, the number of teenagers using oral contraceptives for birth control has been declining. One reason may be side effects, including breast tenderness, break-through bleeding and headaches, which are rare with lower-dose formulations. And the stigma of the pill's early history of health risks lingers on.

"The latest polls do indicate that a number of women and adolescents still harbor fears about birth control pills, as they harbor fears about many contraception methods that are deemed medically safe," said Dr. Vanessa Cullins, vice president for medical affairs at Planned Parenthood.

One persistent concern among women and adolescents is the causal link between oral contraceptives and breast cancer. A 1999 bulletin published by the American College of Obstetricians and Gynecologists identifies this issue as one reason teenagers do not use the pill. Summarizing the findings of more than 50 studies, it stated that "no increased risk of breast cancer" was associated with past oral contraceptive use, "regardless of duration of use."

However, the bulletin noted, controversy continues because one large study has indicated a slightly increased breast cancer risk at a young age related to oral contraceptives.

For Kathy and Lori Rice, the question of the pill's safety was more than academic. "We have a history of gynecological problems and cancer in my family," Kathy Rice said. "My mother had uterine and breast cancer. But Dr. Sucato said she wasn't worried about that because of the low dosage." Lori said she considered the increased risk for breast cancer, and "It worries me a bit."

Weighing her worries against the freedom from her monthly ordeal, she opted for the pill. Slightly more difficult to persuade was Lori's father. "My husband wasn't happy about it," Kathy Rice said. "He's old-fashioned. But Dr. Sucato told him, 'Don't think of it as birth control. Think of it as hormonal therapy.' "

After Long Hiatus, New Contraceptives Emerge

BY LESLIE BERGER | DEC. 10, 2002

AFTER YEARS OF little innovation in birth control, an assortment of new methods offering a broad variety of choices is emerging, including a skin patch that is changed weekly, a hormone-enhanced IUD and a permanent sterilization procedure that requires no anesthesia.

All the new contraceptives are directed at women, and none of them offer proven protection against sexually transmitted diseases. But the new devices offer longer-lasting alternatives to a daily pill and are viewed as long overdue in light of an estimated three million unplanned pregnancies in the United States each year, about half of them ending in abortion.

"We clearly have undermet the need for contraception in the U.S.," said Dr. Lawrence B. Finer, assistant director of research for the Alan Guttmacher Institute, a New York-based nonprofit group that focuses on sexual and reproductive health.

The lack of variety in birth control for Americans can be traced to a tangle of issues, Dr. Finer and other experts said, including the length of time it takes to develop any new medical product and a deeply rooted Puritanical culture. Basic biology has figured in the delay of a long-awaited male pill, since it is easier to suppress one egg a month than millions of sperm all the time.

The chilling effect of controversy has had a role, too. Several experts, including manufacturers, said the current crop of contraceptives were influenced by the stormy history of Norplant, a device that was hailed as the greatest innovation in birth control since the pill, but it was taken off the market in July.

"We learned some lessons from Norplant," said Dr. Trent MacKay, a reproductive health specialist at the National Institutes of Health. "I'm not sure women necessarily got all the counseling they needed about side effects, particularly bleeding side effects. The combination of bleeding and a few other side effects certainly led a lot of women to request removal. And then, as it turned out, at least in some cases, removal was a difficult process."

Introduced to American women in 1991, the Norplant System was a tiny fan of six hormone-releasing cylinders that were planted into the upper arm by a doctor to prevent pregnancy for up to five years.

But the method created by the Population Council, a New York-based research foundation that does most of its work in developing countries, met with immediate criticism in this country. Unpredictable bleeding, rods that became embedded in scar tissue, and fears that the long-acting implant might be used coercively — particularly after a California judge tried to make Norplant a condition of probation — all contributed to its gradual demise.

Then Norplant was the subject of a recall in 2000, stemming from concerns that the hormone-delivery systems of certain lots were defective and could not guarantee contraception. Its distributor, Wyeth Pharmaceuticals, advised patients to use backup methods of birth control and offered to cover the cost of removal.

Finally, in July of this year, Wyeth announced that it would not resume sales of the implant kits and renewed its offer to pay for removals through the end of the year. The decision was folded into a news release stating that the recalled kits had tested effective after all.

Several experts lamented the loss of a birth control option, describing Norplant as a once-promising method that went awry.

"It's a method that has problems, but some women's bodies may adjust to it well," said Barbara Seaman, the feminist health writer who was an early critic of Norplant. "And that's what's so sad about it. I feel so strongly we need to have a great range of methods."

Now the makers of a proposed new implant called Implanon are hoping to capture the market for long-acting contraceptives with only one rod instead of six and a custom-made, disposable inserter to ease insertion and removal. Like Norplant, Implanon uses only progestin,

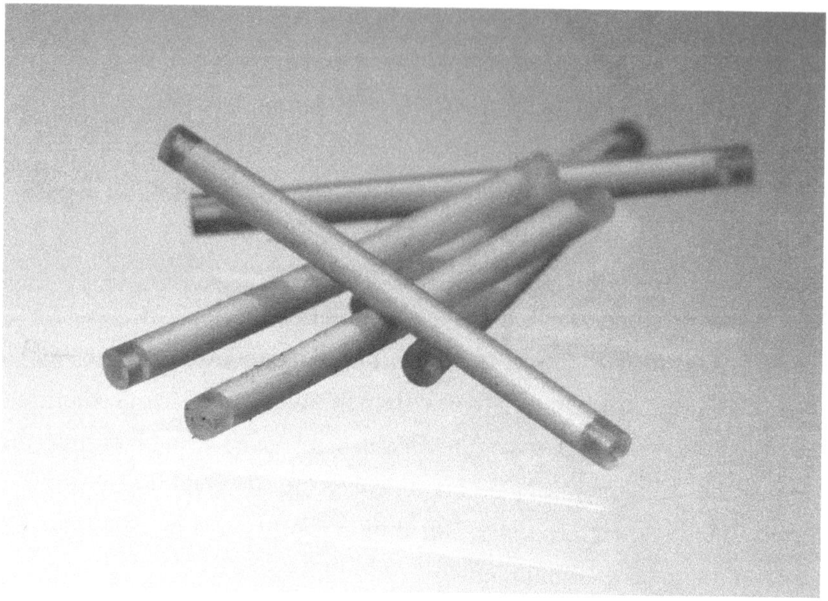

TONY CENICOLA/THE NEW YORK TIMES

After the demise of Norplant, new birth control methods are emerging.

a form of the female hormone progesterone, and can be expected to cause irregular bleeding.

Implanon is also intended to come out after three years rather than five for optimal spacing between children, said Dr. Nancy J. Alexander, director of medical services for Organon USA, the implant's manufacturer.

The company, which is seeking approval of the Food and Drug Administration, hopes to start selling Implanon by early 2004. It is planning elaborate training programs for doctors to avoid the removal problems that plagued Norplant.

"I hope that we won't make the same mistakes," Dr. Alexander said. The makers of the Mirena intrauterine device and the Essure method of sterilization are also emphasizing their nationwide training of doctors and efforts to counsel women.

"We're investing a lot in patient education," said Steven Bacich, the chief executive of Conceptus, a California company that received

F.D.A. approval for Essure in November and has set up an information hotline. "It's the whole issue of trust. You have to establish credibility in the marketplace."

Sterilization is the leading method of birth control, and Essure is the first method for women that can be performed without general anesthesia, Mr. Bacich said. In the brief outpatient procedure, the doctor inserts a narrow catheter and releases a small metal spring into each fallopian tube.

The hormone-free coils stimulate the growth of scar tissue and block the flow of eggs. A kit costs about $950 and the doctors' fee is usually $350 to $500, Mr. Bacich said.

The Mirena IUD, introduced last year by Berlex Laboratories, is reversible but intended to last five years. The IUD emits a progestin that thickens the cervical mucus, making it impenetrable to sperm. It costs about $550.

Pills remain the most popular form of reversible birth control, dominating 97 percent of the market, according to the independent research company IMS Health. But similar combinations of estrogen and progestin in alternative forms are catching on.

The most popular new method is a skin patch that is worn three weeks a month on the abdomen, buttocks or upper body and can be easily changed by the user. Introduced in March, the Ortho Evra patch, by Ortho-McNeil Pharmaceuticals, is already the second most popular form of non-oral birth control in prescriptions and sales, IMS Health figures show, behind Depo-Provera, the 10-year-old contraceptive shot from Pharmacia, given once every three months.

The $30-a-month patch has eclipsed the Lunelle Monthly Contraceptive Injection, a two-year-old shot whose prefilled syringes were recalled in October after a doctor noticed an underfilled syringe. But even before the recall, Lunelle's popularity may have been limited because it can be administered only by a doctor or nurse. "It's a lot for people who have busy lives," said Dr. Laura Corio, a Manhattan

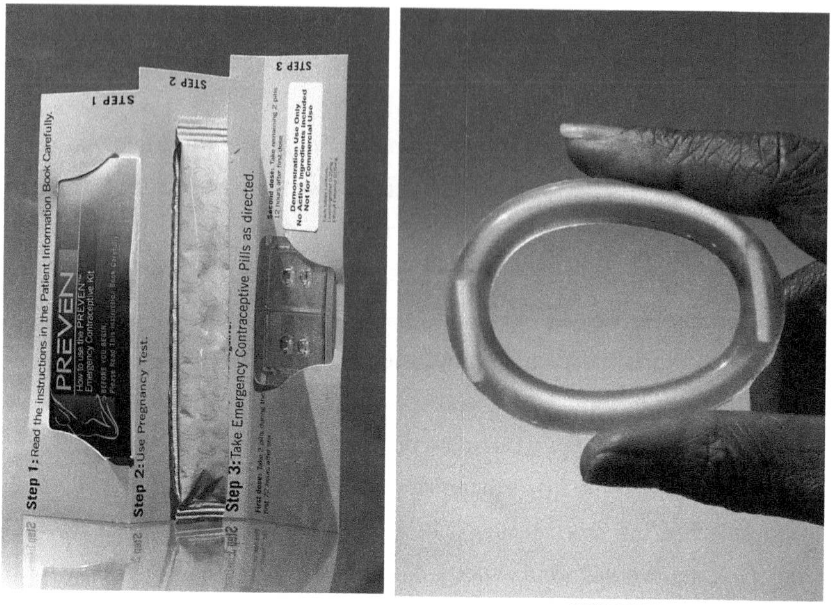

TONY CENICOLA/THE NEW YORK TIMES

Left: emergency pills. Right: a vaginal ring that delivers hormones through the skin.

gynecologist and the author of "The Change Before the Change," dealing with the years before menopause.

Another alternative in the same price range is a small, flexible vaginal ring from Organon called NuvaRing, introduced in June, which also delivers hormones through the skin.

Women can insert it themselves, like a diaphragm, once every three weeks. The steady line of hormones delivered by the new pill alternatives, Dr. Alexander said, is more effective and less nauseating than the hormonal spike and dip that can occur with birth control pills.

Efforts are also under way to make emergency birth control available over the counter. High-dose birth control pills, sold under the names Preven and Plan B, offer immediate backup for women who have had unprotected sex. As an interim measure, Dr. Finer said, California, Washington and Alaska already allow pharmacists to provide the pills to women without a prescription.

The long-term effects of the birth control hormones, which are similar to those used for hormone replacement therapy, continue to be studied.

The Women's Health Initiative, which this summer revealed the risks of a widely used hormone replacement regimen, is continuing to look at the possible cumulative effect of estrogen plus progestin on women who first take them to prevent pregnancy and then at menopause as hormone replacement therapy.

Those data are still being analyzed, said Dr. Margery Gass, a professor of obstetrics and gynecology at the University of Cincinnati and a principal investigator in the hormone replacement study. Results should be released in the next several months, Dr. Gass said.

The eight-year government study of more than 16,000 women over 50 was stopped after five years, when researchers concluded that hormone replacement therapy slightly increased the incidence of breast cancer, heart attacks and strokes.

Still another large government study, Women's CARE, published a month before the hormone replacement report, found that women who took birth control pills at some point in their lives were no more likely to develop breast cancer from ages 35 to 64 than women who had never used oral contraceptives.

The researchers are still trying to determine whether women who took both birth control pills and hormone replacements are at greater risk.

The first generation of women who took the pill in the 1960's are just getting to the age for hormone replacement therapy, "so the jury is still out," said Dr. Robert Spirtas, chief of the National Institutes of Health's contraception and reproductive health branch.

The trend away from barrier methods and toward hormonal contraceptives, which offer no protection against AIDS or other diseases, is a cause for concern but is unlikely to change, said Amy Allina, program and policy director for the National Women's Health Network.

One new hormone-free barrier device is the Lea's Shield, a new cervical cap by Yama Inc., which can be washed and reused for about a year. The caps, approved by the F.D.A. in March, should be available through private doctors in the next two months for about $65 each. About the size of half a lemon, the Lea's Shield does not require fitting because it comes in one size.

By completely covering the cervix, the shield may also offer some protection against sexually transmitted disease, a Yama spokeswoman said. But Ms. Allina warned that this possible benefit of caps and diaphragms, while promising and a subject of growing research, had yet to be proved.

Quest for Male 'Pill' Is Gaining Momentum

BY LESLIE BERGER | DEC. 10, 2002

SCIENTISTS HAVE SUSPECTED since the 1960's, when they invented the birth control pill for women, that manipulating hormones could also suppress the production of sperm.

By giving a synthetic androgen, or male hormone — whether in a pill, an implant or a shot — it is possible to trick the body into halting production of its own testosterone and, in turn, sperm cells.

But finding the lowest effective dose and limiting the side effects have been other matters, ones that have been delayed by skepticism that men will use a hormonal contraceptive and by the reluctance of companies to invest in the research.

Now, recent studies in Britain have shown that a male pill will indeed find a market, mainly among men in monogamous relationships. Moreover, there has been a sharp rise in information, much of it developed through fertility research, about how low sperm levels need to be for a man to be infertile.

A male pill is 5 to 10 years away and is more likely to take the form of an implant or a shot since the most common testosterone taken orally can damage the liver, several experts said. But efforts to develop a male contraceptive are finally gaining momentum, with several clinical trials under way or about to begin.

In the largest study, sponsored by the World Health Organization and the Chinese government, a total of 1,000 men in 10 locations are receiving monthly testosterone injections. Once their sperm counts drop low enough, the participants begin having unprotected sex with their partners.

The short-term side effects of testosterone shots can include acne and weight gain (not in fat but in muscle, like the extra bulk seen in athletes using steroids). But its long-term effects are still largely unknown, so the study's two-year duration is important, said Dr. Christina Wang, a Harbor-U.C.L.A. Medical Center professor and head of the World Health Organization committee overseeing male contraceptive research.

The World Health Organization is negotiating with Schering AG, the German pharmaceutical company, to start another study, this one involving 400 men in Asia, Europe, Australia and the United States. Every two months the men would receive shots of testosterone along with progestin, the female hormone used in birth control pills and other contraceptives. Progestin seems to lower the dose of testosterone and, in turn, temper its effects on the prostate gland, possibly preventing disease, Dr. Wang said.

Another drug company, Organon, is conducting a study combining testosterone shots with progestin implants. "We are seeing which are the best combinations to use," Dr. Wang said.

In smaller studies, the Population Council, an independent research organization, is starting to gauge the effects of an androgen derivative called MENT, an acronym for its chemical formula, developed in the 1960's by the Upjohn Company as an estrogen-suppressing treatment for breast cancer. But it holds more promise as a male contraceptive because it is 10 times as active as testosterone without overstimulating the prostate, Dr. Kalyan Sundaram, a senior scientist at the council, said.

MENT is delivered into the man's body through an implant. It was recently tested in 36 men in Germany, Chile and the Dominican Republic, and now is being studied in 72 men in Germany, Chile and Los Angeles, Dr. Sundaram said. The new study combines MENT with progestin.

Schering AG is also experimenting with MENT in a gel form as a possible hormone therapy for men with abnormally low levels of testosterone.

The hormone replacement therapy could be on the market in five years, said Dr. Elof D. B. Johansson, the Population Council's vice president. But a MENT contraceptive is at least 10 years away, he said.

"Male physiology conspires against an easy solution," Dr. Nancy J. Alexander, medical services director for Organon USA, wrote in a 1999 article in Scientific American. While fertile women produce a single egg a month on a predictable cycle, men produce tens of millions of sperm every day in the testes. Since it takes about 75 days for sperm cells to mature and become capable of fertilizing an egg, any contraceptive aimed at sperm production needs at least two and a half months to work.

Chinese scientists thought they had found an answer in the 1970's with gossypol, the active ingredient derived from cottonseed oil, after they realized that poor rural families who cooked with it had lower birth rates. A yellow compound whose effects were greatest when its color was brightest, gossypol pills suppressed fertility by damaging the testes. But it caused unacceptably low potassium levels and irreversible infertility in some men, Dr. Alexander said.

Researchers then tried gossypol in a vaginal cream. That proved an effective contraceptive, she said, but marketing efforts ended because the compound's intense and essential color stained bedsheets.

Catholic Group Is Told to Pay for Birth Control

BY STEPHANIE STROM | MARCH 2, 2004

THE CALIFORNIA SUPREME COURT ruled Monday that Catholic Charities must provide its employees in California with medical coverage for birth control, in spite of its religious objections to contraception.

The ruling has sweeping implications for religion-based nonprofit organizations and hospitals throughout the state and could influence decisions made in at least 20 other states that have similar laws requiring employers to provide contraception as part of employee health coverage, legal experts said. A similar case, brought by Catholic and Protestant organizations, is winding its way through the New York courts.

"There are other groups in similar situations in California, so it is quite significant in that way," said Erwin Chemerinsky, a law professor at the University of Southern California. "And it probably will influence how the laws are interpreted in other states. It's an important ruling."

Ned Dolejsi, executive director of the California Catholic Conference, said the court's decision was a sign of the times.

"We're very disappointed in the ruling and sad that this is apparently an indication of where our society is at this time in terms of its respect for religious diversity," Mr. Dolejsi said.

The United States Supreme Court has narrowed its protection of religious practices, a move legal scholars attribute to its reluctance to force judges to weigh the relative merits of church and state interests.

"This is a shocking interference with internal church affairs, but it's the way the law has been headed broadly," said Douglas Laycock, a law professor at the University of Texas. "They shouldn't be able to do this, because as a matter of principle this is just wrong, but cases have been going this way."

Catholic Charities of Sacramento, which brought the case in 2000, argued that it should be exempt from the state law because it is a unit of the Roman Catholic Church, and the law does allow an exemption for "religious employers" like churches.

But the State Supreme Court ruled that the organization did not meet any of the criteria defining a religious employer under the law, which was passed in 1999. Under that definition, an employer must be primarily engaged in spreading religious values, employ mostly people who hold the religious beliefs of the organization, serve largely people with the same religious beliefs, and be a nonprofit religious organization as defined under the federal tax code.

Mr. Dolejsi said the court had either ignored or misunderstood the relationship between Catholic Charities and the Roman Catholic Church.

"Every Catholic Charities is part of the Catholic diocese in the area where it is," he said. "Officially and formally, Catholic Charities of Sacramento is part of the Catholic Church in Sacramento, answerable to the local bishop and providing the services the church provides as a religious organization."

Most of the Catholic Charities organizations in California have been providing contraceptive coverage as required by law pending the outcome of the suit, Mr. Dolejsi said, adding that they did so "under protest."

The law does provide an exception for employers, who are only required to provide coverage for birth control if they offer their employees a prescription drug benefits plan.

Mr. Dolejsi said he did not know if Catholic Charities would use that technicality, which he said would violate its commitment to providing a just workplace.

"The court is forcing us to choose between our religious beliefs," he said.

Proponents of laws requiring employers to provide contraception as part of their health benefits packages hailed the decision.

"It is a strong affirmation of the most basic principles of fairness for women and a recognition as well that women's reproductive health care can't be treated in a second-class way," said Marcia D. Greenberger, president of the National Women's Law Center, an advocacy group.

Ms. Greenberger noted that the lone dissenter in the California decision was Justice Janice Rogers Brown, whose nomination to the United States Court of Appeals for the District of Columbia by President Bush has been opposed by some Democratic senators who consider her too conservative. President Bush has pushed for greater public support for religion-based organizations like Catholic Charities, many of which provide vital social services like homeless shelters and medical clinics without proselytizing.

In her dissent, Justice Brown said the California Legislature had too narrowly defined "religious employers" if organizations like Catholic Charities did not qualify. "Here we are dealing with an intentional, purposeful intrusion into a religious organization's expression of its religious tenets and sense of mission," she wrote.

Morning-After-Pill Ruling Defies Norm

BY GARDINER HARRIS | MAY 8, 2004

A TOP FEDERAL DRUG official said yesterday that he rejected not only the judgment of an advisory panel but also the recommendations of his own staff when he refused to allow a morning-after pill to be sold over the counter.

Dr. Steven Galson, acting director of the Food and Drug Administration's center for drug evaluation and research since October, acknowledged in an interview that his action was not the norm.

"I am not trying to convey this decision as being common or usual," Dr. Galson said.

The morning-after pill, called Plan B, is an emergency birth-control medicine that is currently sold only by prescription. Made of high-dose birth-control pills, it can interfere with ovulation and perhaps prevent a fertilized egg from being implanted if taken within 72 hours of unprotected sex.

The pill's maker, Barr Pharmaceuticals, hopes to sell it over the counter, a prospect that seemed likely in December when a federal advisory panel voted 23 to 4 to approve Barr's application. The agency normally follows the recommendations of its advisory panels, especially when their votes are overwhelming. Barr's hopes were raised even further when Dr. Galson's staff similarly recommended approval.

But on Thursday, the agency sent Barr a "nonapprovable" letter, saying it had rejected the company's application because it did not provide enough information about how young teenagers would be able to use the drug properly.

In interviews yesterday, several former F.D.A. officials said that they could not remember another instance in which Dr. Galson, a career officer in the public health service, or any of his predecessors had overruled both an advisory committee and staff recommendations.

"I can't ever remember the center director ever signing a nonapprovable letter," said Dr. Raymond Lipicky, who retired from a top agency position in 2002 after 18 years in the agency. "In my experience, that never happened." Such letters are invariably issued at a much lower level than the director.

Dr. Robert R. Fenichel, who left the agency in 2000 after 12 years, said, "This is simply unheard of."

Their comments came in the midst of a fierce debate about whether the agency's decision was based primarily in science or politics.

Dr. Galson said he knew of just a single instance in the past 10 years in which one of his predecessors had overruled the conclusions of those below him. "This isn't common, but it's not unheard of," he said.

Dr. Galson did not just disagree a little bit with his staff and the advisory board. If he had, he would have suggested that Barr receive an "approvable" letter for its application. Such a letter tells a company that it could receive approval if it provides certain additional information.

Despite its cheery name, such letters are not good news for companies, some of which have worked for years to develop and provide the information requested. Still, they are better than "nonapprovable" letters like the one Dr. Galson decided to send to Barr. Such letters suggest that approval is unlikely, companies say.

By sending a nonapprovable letter, Dr. Galson said in the interview, "We said that the shortcomings are so large that we are not able to go that intermediary step."

He said Barr had failed to prove that girls younger than 17 could use Plan B safely without the help of a physician, because the company's study included just 29 girls younger than 17 and none younger than 14. He said he worried that such girls might be more likely to have sex without condoms — exposing themselves to an increased risk of disease — if they had easier access to Plan B.

"The worse-case scenario is that you've got a young couple and they would normally use a condom when they were having intercourse, but since they know they can run to the CVS to get Plan B, are they going to worry about that?" he asked.

Conservative groups endorsed the action.

"This is a prudent decision to say that we must consider the consequences if teens use this drug as a means of birth control," said Tony Perkins, president of the Family Research Council, a conservative group.

But the agency's decision to take into account how some people might change their behavior because a drug is more available is also unprecedented, critics charge. Dr. Scott Spear of the Planned Parenthood Federation of America, noted that the agency was unlikely to ask the makers of anticholesterol pills if people would eat more cheeseburgers when their drugs became available over the counter.

"It's a bogus issue," Dr. Spear said. "They should be asking if the drug is safe and whether it's effective. That's it."

But Wendy Wright, senior policy director at Concerned Women for America, a conservative group, said the agency's questions were entirely appropriate. "One cheeseburger is not going to kill you, while risky sex can be life-threatening in one instance," she said.

Moralists at the Pharmacy

EDITORIAL | BY THE NEW YORK TIMES | APRIL 3, 2005

SCATTERED REPORTS SUGGEST that a growing number of pharmacists around the country are refusing to fill prescriptions for contraceptives or morning-after birth control pills because of moral or religious objections. Although the refusals are cast as important matters of conscience for self-described "pro-life" pharmacists, they have the pernicious effect of delaying, and sometimes even denying, a woman's access to medications that may be urgently needed. This is an intolerable abuse of power by pharmacists who have no business forcing their own moral or ethical views onto customers who may not share them. Any pharmacist who cannot dispense medicines lawfully prescribed by a doctor should find another line of work.

Incidents in which pharmacists have refused to dispense contraceptives or morning-after pills have been reported for well over a decade, but the number may be rising. By one count there were some 180 reports of refusals in a six-month period last year, some describing earlier incidents, and the number is likely to grow now that religious conservatives are flexing their muscles in many spheres of life.

An organization of antiabortion pharmacists is pushing for professional associations and state legislatures to adopt "conscience clauses" recognizing the pharmacist's right to refuse to dispense a drug or even refer the customer to a pharmacist who will; many pharmacy associations have already adopted such clauses. Several states have laws granting pharmacists the right to refuse, and legislators in at least 10 states are pushing similar legislation.

Meanwhile, legislators in other states are trying to force pharmacists to fill valid prescriptions, and Gov. Rod Blagojevich of Illinois, responding to a Chicago pharmacist's recent refusal to provide contraceptives to two women, issued a rule on Friday that pharmacies must fill contraceptive prescriptions without delay. The nationwide struggle was described in a Washington Post article last Monday.

The most responsible conscience clauses try to balance the rights of the pharmacist and the rights of the clients by insisting that steps be taken to ensure patient access to legally prescribed therapy, either through another pharmacist at the same store or through another pharmacy. That may seem at first blush like a reasonable compromise but it is a prescription for disaster in the real world.

To begin with, some pharmacists are so certain of their moral high ground that they berate, belittle or lecture their customers. They are not likely to be helpful in guiding patients to alternative supplies of medications that they deem evil. Worse yet, if this movement picks up steam, right-to-life groups in some areas may pressure one pharmacy after another to refuse service, leaving a diminished pool of pharmacies available to fill prescriptions for birth control purposes. It is disheartening that Wal-Mart, for some years now, has refused to stock the morning-after pill.

In rural areas there may not be another pharmacy nearby, so customers who are turned away may go without the medication or waste time finding another pharmacy. In the case of the morning-after pills, which work best in the first 12 to 24 hours after a sexual encounter, delay could render the treatment ineffective. Indeed, pharmacists who refuse to fill prescriptions for morning-after pills are inadvertently strengthening the case for providing them as nonprescription medicines on the open shelves. Such availability would allow women to get the pills promptly without going first to a doctor and then to a potentially obstructionist pharmacist.

CHAPTER 6

Acceptance and Renewed Attacks

In recent years, birth control has become an accepted and normal aspect of daily life. Many teenagers are encouraged to practice "safe sex," and young women can talk to their doctors and be prescribed birth control pills for free under the Affordable Care Act. And, yet, there continue to be political attacks against the accessibility of birth control. In recent years, organizations on the political right have argued that providing birth control to all violates certain individuals' "religious liberty." This means that they disagree with birth control on a religious basis and should not be forced — as doctors, prescribers or owners of companies — to provide birth control against their personal beliefs. Many women, however, view birth control availability as an issue of women's, and indeed human, rights.

Promises the Pill Could Never Keep

OPINION | BY ELAINE TYLER MAY | APRIL 24, 2010

MINNEAPOLIS — An end to poverty. A cure for divorce. The elimination of unwed pregnancy. Fifty years ago next month, when the Food and Drug Administration announced that it would approve the oral contraceptive, these were the highest expectations for it. At the same time, few of its promoters in 1960 imagined how the pill, as it quickly became known, would become a powerful tool for transforming women's lives.

In 1954, John Rock, the doctor who was leading the research on the pill, expressed the breathless excitement shared by many of his colleagues: An oral contraceptive, he said, "would be the greatest aid ever discovered to the happiness and security of individual families — indeed, to mankind" because "the greatest menace to world peace and decent standards of life today is not atomic energy but sexual energy."

At an international medical conference in Bombay a few years after F.D.A. approval, another doctor unfurled a rolled package of birth control pills into the packed auditorium and announced that the pill would solve India's problems of hunger and poverty by leveling off its population. As it turned out, the pill had little effect on India's or any other developing country's population — because most women lacked access to medical clinics that could provide them with prescriptions and follow-up exams.

In the United States, some people claimed the pill would free married couples from fears of unwanted pregnancy, improving their sex lives and lowering the divorce rate. "With my wife on the pill, any moment is the right moment for love," one euphoric husband said in 1969. "Unpremeditated sex is marvelous!"

Not every husband, though, found the pill quite so beneficial. Dr. Robert W. Kistner, a doctor at Harvard who was an early advocate of the pill, wrote in Ladies' Home Journal: "Many wives feel sexually liberated by birth-control pills. But some husbands feel enslaved. It's as if their sense of maleness and self-esteem has been threatened." Kistner warned that "if the wives assumed the dominant role in the sex act or became the least bit animalistic," husbands might become impotent.

Whether men found the pill a boon for or a deterrent to their sex lives, the annual divorce rate more than doubled in the 1960s and '70s from 9 of every 1,000 married women to 23.

Others predicted that the pill would prevent pregnancy among "naughty little girls," Rock's description of sexually active single women. But the pill did not prevent unwed pregnancy, which in 1980 increased to 18 percent of all births, from 5 percent in 1960. Until 1972, several states barred the prescribing of contraceptives to unmarried women, and even where it was legal, many women were afraid to ask their doctors for the pill. In any case, as late as 1972, three-fourths of sexually active young, single women rarely or never used any form of birth control, a national study showed.

Just as the optimists were wrong about the pill's effect on population, marriage and unwed pregnancy, so were pessimists who feared that the pill would unleash some kind of sexual chaos. A 1966 article in U.S. News and World Report asked, "What is the pill doing to the moral patterns of the nation?" and "Is the pill regarded as a license for promiscuity? Can its availability to all women of childbearing age lead to sexual anarchy?"

The answers turned out to be negative. The "sexual revolution" began largely among college students in the 1950s, before the pill was available, and did not reach the mainstream until the late 1960s. In 1968, Science News reported that despite the "flood tide of publicity over oral contraception and its moral impact," the pill had little effect on the sexual behavior of unmarried men and women. One doctor at the time explained it this way: "The presence of the pill does not make people decide to have sex. It is after they decide to have sex that they go get the pill."

In spite of all the missed predictions, there were at least two people who understood the pill's revolutionary potential from the beginning: Margaret Sanger, who had first imagined a contraceptive pill in 1912, and Katharine McCormick, a wealthy feminist — both elderly women who had been advocates for women's rights since the early 20th century, and who teamed up in the 1950s to bring the pill project to fruition. Sanger and McCormick financed the research and found the scientists to conduct it.

Sanger and McCormick anticipated how the pill would be a tool for women's emancipation. And, indeed, the minute the F.D.A. announced it would be approved, millions of women rushed to their doctors for prescriptions. They would use the pill to gain control of not only their fertility, but also their lives. They could decide whether to have children, and when. They could take advantage of new opportunities for education, work and participation in public life that opened up in the years following the pill's approval.

Today, women no longer need to choose between having a family and a career. At the pill's 50th anniversary, that alone is well worth celebrating.

ELAINE TYLER MAY, a professor of history at the University of Minnesota, is the author, most recently, of the forthcoming "America and the Pill."

What Every Girl Should Know

OPINION | BY GAIL COLLINS | MAY 7, 2010

A THOUSAND YEARS AGO, popular birth control methods in the Western world included spitting into the mouth of a frog, eating bees and wearing the testicles of a weasel. In Córdoba, Spain, which was supposed to be on the scientific cutting edge, women were told to leap up and down vigorously after sex, and then jump backward nine times.

This is by way of saying that on Sunday we celebrate the 50th anniversary of the birth control pill. We live in troubled times. But let's give thanks that we avoided the era of the weasel testicles.

Like a great many of our anniversaries, this one is a movable feast. The Food and Drug Administration actually gave G.D. Searle the go-ahead to market the first oral contraceptive (not counting bees) on June 23, 1960. But the F.D.A. announced its intention to approve the pill on May 9, which also happens to be Mother's Day this year and, therefore, too good to resist.

This is a story about science, and obviously sex. But it's also a saga about getting information.

American women had been limiting the size of their families long before the pill came along. In the 19th century, the fertility rate was plummeting, and ads for everything from condoms to douching syringes helped keep urban newspapers solvent. My favorite factoid from this period is that a company called National Syringe offered a model with changeable nozzles so it could be used for both birth control and watering plants.

What women did not have was the ability to figure out what actually worked. The powers-that-be believed that the only appropriate form of birth control was celibacy. "Can they not use self control?" demanded Anthony Comstock, the powerful crusader for the Sexual Purity campaign. "Or must they sink to the level of the beasts?"

TONY CENICOLA/THE NEW YORK TIMES

Gail Collins.

Comstock managed to get New York authorities to grant him the powers to both arrest and censor, and he bragged that he sent 4,000 people to jail for helping women understand, and use, birth control. He seemed to take particular pleasure in the fact that 15 of them had committed suicide.

One of his targets was Margaret Sanger, a nurse who wrote a sex education column, "What Every Girl Should Know," for a left-wing New York newspaper, The Call. When Comstock banned her column on venereal disease, the paper ran an empty space with the title: "What Every Girl Should Know: Nothing, by Order of the U.S. Post Office."

Sanger was the first person to publish an evaluation of all the available forms of birth control. As a reward, she got a criminal obscenity charge. She fled to Europe to avoid going to jail, and her husband was imprisoned for passing out one of her pamphlets. In the end, he got 30 days, and Anthony Comstock got a chill during the trial that led to a fatal case of pneumonia.

It was the courts that eventually gave women the right to not only have access to birth control, but also information that told them what was available and how to use it. (The first big victory had the memorable name of U.S. v. One Package of Japanese Pessaries.) Sanger, meanwhile, helped bring together the wealthy donors and brilliant researchers who would bring forth the first effective oral contraception.

"There's gonna be some changes made right here on Nursery Hill," sang Loretta Lynn. "You've set this chicken your last time 'cause now I've got the pill."

And we lived happily ever after. Except that over the last 20 years, protests from the social right have made politicians frightened of mentioning birth control and school boards frightened of including it in the curriculum.

Cecile Richards, the president of Planned Parenthood, remembers getting a pretty thorough grounding in sex and the ways to prevent pregnancy when she was in school — back in the days when the raciest thing you saw on television was Rob and Laura Petrie waking up in twin beds on the opposite side of the room. "Kids growing up today watch 'Gossip Girl' and all these shows where every teenager is having sex every day — and now we don't teach sex education in school," she noted.

Even though 100 million women take the pill every day, to the great relief of 100 million or so of their partners, the terror of mentioning birth control is so great that the humongous new health care reform act has managed to avoid bringing it up at all. Advocates are hoping that when the regulations are finally written, they will require health insurance to cover birth control pills like any other drug. But nobody is sure.

"If the administration would announce tomorrow that all birth control would be free for every woman in America, I think the health care plan would gain 30 points in popularity overnight," said Richards.

GAIL COLLINS is an Op-Ed columnist for The New York Times.

Poverty and the Pill

OPINION | BY NICHOLAS KRISTOF | MAY 19, 2010

KINSHASA, CONGO — Earthquakes are more dramatic. Tsunamis make better television. AIDS is more visceral.

But here's a far more widespread challenge, one that's also more fixable: the unavailability of birth control in many poor countries. I'm on my annual win-a-trip journey across a chunk of Central Africa with a 19-year-old university student, Mitch Smith. He won the right to bounce over impossible roads in the region where it's easy to see firsthand how breakneck population growth is linked to poverty, instability and conflict.

In almost every village we stop in, we chat with families whose huts overflow with small children — whom the parents can't always afford to educate, feed or protect from disease.

Here in Kinshasa, we met Emilie Lunda, 25, who had nearly died during childbirth a few days earlier. Doctors saved her life, but her baby died. And she is still recuperating in a hospital and doesn't know how she will pay the bill.

"I didn't want to get pregnant," Emilie told us here in the Congolese capital. "I was afraid of getting pregnant." But she had never heard of birth control.

In rural parts of Congo Republic, the other Congo to the north, we found that even when people had heard of contraception, they often regarded it as unaffordable.

Most appalling, all the clinics and hospitals we visited in Congo Republic said that they would sell contraceptives only to women who brought their husbands in with them to prove that the husband accepted birth control.

Condoms are somewhat easier to obtain, but many men resist them. More broadly, many men seem to feel that more children are a proud sign of more virility.

So the pill, 50 years old this month in the United States, has yet to reach parts of Africa. And condoms and other forms of birth control and AIDS prevention are still far too difficult to obtain in some areas.

America's widely respected Guttmacher Institute, which conducts research on reproductive health, says that 215 million women around the world are sexually active and don't want to become pregnant — but are not using modern forms of contraception.

Making contraception available to all these women worldwide would cost less than $4 billion, Guttmacher said in an important study published last year. That's about what the United States is spending every two weeks on our military force in Afghanistan.

What's more, each dollar spent on contraception would actually reduce total medical spending by $1.40 by reducing sums spent on unplanned births and abortions, the study said.

If contraception were broadly available in poor countries, the report said, more than 50 million unwanted pregnancies could be averted annually. One result would be 25 million fewer abortions per year. Another would be saving the lives of as many as 150,000 women who now die annually in childbirth.

Family planning has stalled since the 1980s. Republican administrations cut off all American financing for the United Nations Population Fund, the main international agency supporting family-planning programs. Paradoxically, conservative hostility to some family-planning programs almost certainly resulted in more abortions.

The Obama administration has restored that financing, and it should make a priority of broader access to contraception (and to girls' education, which may be the most effective contraceptive of all).

In fairness, family planning is harder than it looks. Many impoverished men and women, especially those without education, want babies more than contraceptives. As Mitch and I drove through villages, we asked many women how many babies they would ideally have. Most said five or six, and a few said 10.

Parents want many children partly because they expect some to die. So mosquito nets, vaccinations and other steps to reduce child mortality also help to create an environment where family planning is more readily accepted.

In short, what's needed is a comprehensive approach to assisting men and women alike with family planning — not just a contraceptive dispensary.

Romerchinelle Mietala, a 17-year-old girl in Mindouli, Congo Republic, has one baby and told us that she doesn't really want another child for now. But she had never heard of contraceptives and, when we explained, was ambivalent. She worried about her status in the village if she didn't get pregnant again reasonably soon.

"If a woman doesn't have a baby every two or three years, people will say she's sterile," she said.

Another woman in Mindouli, Christine Kanda, said that she is ready to stop now after eight children — two of which have died. But she doesn't know if her husband will accompany her to the clinic to sign off, and she doesn't know how she would pay the $1 a month that the hospital charges.

So she may just keep on producing babies.

NICHOLAS KRISTOF is an Op-Ed columnist for The New York Times.

Let the Pill Go Free

OPINION | BY KELLY BLANCHARD | JUNE 21, 2010

LAST MONTH, THE 50th anniversary of the Food and Drug Administration's approval of the birth control pill was marked by a lot of discussion about the ways in which the pill has failed to deliver on its promises. It did not solve women's problems juggling work and family life — nor did it end gender discrimination or eliminate unintended pregnancies. Clearly, approving the use of the pill was only the beginning of the effort to meet women's contraception needs.

The pill remains part of the solution, but its usefulness has been limited because it's available only by prescription. As every woman who has run out of pills on a Sunday or forgotten to take them along on vacation knows, refills are not always easy to come by.

What's more, the difficulties involved in obtaining a pill prescription, especially for women without access to a doctor, can cause gaps in contraceptive use. And the birth control methods that are available without prescription — condoms, spermicide and the sponge — have higher failure rates than the pill.

But there is something we could do to help the pill live up to its potential: let women purchase it over the counter. A half-century of evidence shows us that it's safe to dispense the pill without a prescription.

The pill meets F.D.A. criteria for over-the-counter medications. Women don't need a doctor to tell them whether they need the pill — they know when they are sexually active and want to avoid pregnancy. Pill instructions are easy to follow: Take one each day. There's no chance of becoming addicted. Taking too many will make you nauseated, but won't endanger your life, in contrast to some over-the-counter drugs, like analgesics. (There are even side benefits to taking the pill, like reduced risks of ovarian and uterine cancer.)

It's true that the pill could be dangerous for women with certain conditions. Women who are 35 or older and smoke, and those with high blood pressure, are at greater risk of a heart attack or stroke if they take oral contraceptives that combine estrogen and progestin. But these are not complicated conditions to identify; women already have to tell their doctor about their health problems when they get a prescription, and research shows that women can screen themselves for contraindications almost as well as providers do.

Progestin-only pills, or minipills, might be an ideal option for an initial over-the-counter switch since they have fewer (and rarer) contraindications and potential complications. Along with the change, the pharmaceutical company, nonprofits and the government should collaborate on an educational campaign, including pamphlets packaged with the pills and public service announcements that would give women information about how to use the pill, deal with side effects, recognize serious complications and of course remind them to get regular checkups for preventative care like Pap smears.

The United States has one of the highest teenage pregnancy rates in the developed world, and better access to the pill is part of the solution to this problem. During the debate leading up to F.D.A. approval of the emergency contraception pill called Plan B for over-the-counter sale, some people expressed concern about expanding access to contraception for young women without doctors' oversight, and they might say the same about the birth control pill. But there are no special health risks for younger women on the pill, and sexually active women, whatever their age, should have freer access to the full range of options to prevent pregnancy.

We also need to address the problem of pricing. Plan B became more expensive when it went over the counter. If that happened to the pill, it could be unaffordable for many women on Medicaid whose prescriptions are now covered. In some states Medicaid already covers over-the-counter contraception like condoms; Medicaid coverage in all states should be extended to all over-the-counter methods, including the pill.

Women don't need a doctor to tell them if they need cold medicine or condoms, and they shouldn't need a doctor's permission to take the pill. Over-the-counter sales would expand access to safe, effective contraception, and help women take control over their sexual and reproductive lives.

KELLY BLANCHARD is the president of Ibis Reproductive Health, a nonprofit research organization.

Morning-After Pill Is Not a Cure-All

BY RONI CARYN RABIN | APRIL 8, 2013

IF A RECENT federal court ruling stands, any young woman will be able to walk into her neighborhood drugstore, find the morning-after pill near the shelves stocked with condoms and KY Jelly and buy it — no questions asked.

That would be a surprising change: At the moment, girls 16 and younger must have a prescription to buy the morning-after pill, which helps prevent pregnancy after sexual intercourse. As a result, even though it is nonprescription for everyone else, even an older woman can buy it only at the pharmacy window, and she must show a valid ID and proof of age.

Scientists at the Food and Drug Administration and at numerous professional medical societies have long endorsed easier access to Plan B, the most common brand of emergency contraception. But in 2011, Kathleen Sebelius, the secretary of health and human services, took the unusual step of countermanding a move by the F.D.A. to make the pill universally available.

On Friday, a federal judge in New York State gave the agency 30 days to lift age and sale restrictions on Plan B and its generic versions. Nancy Northup, president of the Center for Reproductive Rights, a legal advocacy group that sued to expand nonprescription access to Plan B, called the ruling "a resounding triumph for science over politics."

The irony is that despite the long legal battle to make the morning-after pill more widely available, greater access to Plan B is not likely to have a dramatic impact. It's unlikely to trigger another sexual revolution, change sexual mores, or even to reduce pregnancy rates among unmarried women, most observers agree.

Studies have suggested that many women are not aware that there even is a morning-after pill. Plan B is expensive, about $50, and many women could find the price alone a deterrent. If drugstores choose to keep Plan B locked up, teenagers may be reluctant to ask for it.

Moreover, Plan B is not a panacea. While it is most effective when taken within days or hours of unprotected intercourse, it doesn't always work.

Still, Plan B and another option, Next Choice, were effective in at least half of the instances they were used, according to one review of published data. And some studies have found that the drugs are just as effective two to four days after unprotected sex as they are when taken the next day.

Even when the morning-after pill was made available in advance to young women in clinical studies, however, they often did not use it and pregnancy rates were not affected. Older girls were just as likely to use other forms of birth control, though some studies found that younger girls from troubled backgrounds said they were more careless when given access to a morning-after pill.

Compared with years past, American teenagers have been postponing sexual activity, beginning sex on average at 17. Teenage childbearing rates have dropped sharply in the past 50 years. At the same time, more than half of births to women under the age of 30 now occur outside marriage, according to government data.

"This is not a magic bullet," said Dr. Susan Wood, an associate professor of health policy at George Washington University. "It's just one more tool in the toolbox — one more option that can help women have that second chance if they need it."

Conservative opponents continue to raise questions about the drug's mechanism, calling it a possible abortifacient, although the scientific consensus is that the morning-after pill is a contraceptive that prevents pregnancy by interfering with ovulation and not with implantation of a fertilized egg.

Dr. Mary Davenport, recent president of the American Association of Pro-Life Obstetricians and Gynecologists, acknowledged that her group's opposition to Plan B is rooted in broader concerns about casual sexual activity, teenage pregnancy and single motherhood.

"Fear of pregnancy is a deterrent to sexual activity," Dr. Davenport said. "When you introduce something like this, it changes people's behaviors, and they have more risky sex. Teens will be counting on this morning-after pill to bail them out, and they'll have more casual encounters."

Giving minors direct access to Plan B also takes parents, guardians and other responsible adults like physicians out of the equation at a time when young women may need their help and advice, she said.

The next legal step is not clear. Justice Department officials have not said yet whether they will appeal the decision.

Ms. Northup said all eyes were now on President Obama, who has championed contraception coverage as an essential component of health care reform and, despite the controversy surrounding this issue, made it a required element of employer-provided health insurance under the Affordable Care Act.

"Whether we're talking about emergency contraceptives or aspirin, the standard should be whether it is safe and effective for people to use without a prescription," Ms. Northup said. "This is very safe. You can't misuse emergency contraception. Why in this area are we asking for a different standard?"

Insurers Flout Rule Covering Birth Control, Studies Find

BY ROBERT PEAR | APRIL 29, 2015

WASHINGTON — Health insurance companies often flout a federal requirement that they cover all approved methods of birth control for women without co-payments or other charges, a major benefit of the Affordable Care Act, two new studies have found.

Responding to the reports, senior Democratic members of Congress prodded the White House on Wednesday to step up enforcement of the requirement. Senator Patty Murray of Washington, the senior Democrat on the Senate health committee, said she was "extremely disappointed" by the findings, and she asked Sylvia Mathews Burwell, the secretary of health and human services, to investigate the problems reported by many women.

Guidelines issued by the federal government in 2011 require insurers to provide women with coverage at no cost for all methods of contraception approved by the Food and Drug Administration. Insurers are also supposed to provide free coverage for sterilization procedures and "patient education and counseling for all women with reproductive capacity."

But a report issued on Wednesday by the National Women's Law Center, a nonprofit group that lobbied for the benefit, and a separate report issued this month by the Kaiser Family Foundation found that cost was a significant barrier to some forms of birth control for some women.

"The promise of the Affordable Care Act has not become a reality," said Gretchen Borchelt, a vice president of the women's law center, reporting on a review of health plan documents in 15 states and hundreds of calls to the center's toll-free help line. "Insurance companies are still not providing coverage for all F.D.A.-approved methods of birth control, or they impose out-of-pocket costs on them."

Women "may end up going without the care they need even though they have health insurance," she said.

The food and drug agency has approved 20 distinct methods of birth control, but the researchers found that some insurers lumped together several methods of contraception and covered only one or two in a category. For example, they said, some insurers did not cover the contraceptive patch or the vaginal contraceptive ring because they covered another "hormonal method" of contraception: birth control pills.

Likewise, they said, some plans declined to provide free contraceptive coverage to women over a certain age. And some, they found, covered low-cost generic versions of birth control drugs, but not brand-name versions.

Ms. Burwell said the Obama administration would clarify its guidelines for state insurance regulators. Katie Hill, a spokeswoman for Ms. Burwell, said, "We take reports of noncompliance very seriously." The federal government runs the public insurance marketplace in more than 30 states.

Representative Rosa DeLauro, Democrat of Connecticut, said: "The rules prohibiting cost-sharing on preventive care, including contraception, are clear, and insurers who are not following them are in violation of the law. Insurance companies need to come into compliance immediately. The Department of Health and Human Services and state regulators need to crack down on those who do not."

But Karen M. Ignagni, the president of America's Health Insurance Plans, said the law center's report provided "a distorted picture of reality."

"Health plans provide access to care for millions of women each day and receive high marks in customer satisfaction surveys," Ms. Ignagni said.

When insurers limit coverage or charge co-payments, they often say that they are using "reasonable medical management techniques," as permitted by federal rules.

The Kaiser foundation examined plans offered by 20 insurers in five states. It found that five charged co-payments for the NuvaRing contraceptive and that one did not cover the ring at all. In addition, it said, three carriers required women to pay some of the cost for the contraceptive patch.

Kaiser also found that some plans charged for the patch or the ring, or did not cover them at all, on the ground that they had "the same chemical formulation" as birth control pills.

Matthew N. Wiggin, a spokesman for Aetna, said the company was committed to complying with the law and now "covers each method of contraception," having added coverage of Merck's NuvaRing this year.

Karen Eldred, a spokeswoman for Cigna, said, "We provide access to all generic contraceptives." Women, she said, are normally expected to share in the cost of the NuvaRing, but a provider "may call Cigna Pharmacy to obtain no-cost coverage" if the doctor believes it is "medically appropriate."

Senator Richard Blumenthal, Democrat of Connecticut, said he shared the concerns expressed in the reports. "Strong sanctions should apply to any insurer that shirks its legal and moral duties," he said.

After Health Care Act, Sharp Drop in Spending on Birth Control

BY SABRINA TAVERNISE | JULY 7, 2015

OUT-OF-POCKET SPENDING on most major birth control methods fell sharply in the months after the Affordable Care Act began requiring insurance plans to cover contraception at no cost to women, a new study has found. Spending on the pill, the most popular form of prescription birth control, dropped by about half in the first six months of 2013, compared with the same period in 2012, before the mandate took effect.

The study, by health economists from the University of Pennsylvania, analyzed health insurance claims from a large private insurer with business in all 50 states and the District of Columbia. It evaluated the effect of the Affordable Care Act, the biggest piece of social legislation in decades, on women's pocketbooks. It estimated that savings from the pill alone were about $1.4 billion in 2013.

Cost has long been a major obstacle to women getting birth control, and declines in what they pay for contraceptives have the potential to increase access and reduce unplanned pregnancies. About half of the 6.6 million pregnancies a year in the United States are unintended, far higher than in most developed countries.

The study, published online in Health Affairs on Tuesday, was not able to definitively establish whether the law drove women's falling expenditures on birth control, but experts said the magnitude and timing of the decline suggested that it was.

Researchers who led the study took a random sample from a private database of millions of patients — about 790,000 women from 13 to 45 — and analyzed their contraceptive use from 2008 to 2013. The data was leased by the University of Pennsylvania on the condition that the insurer not be identified.

Experts cautioned that the sample, while large, represented claims from just one insurer and was not designed to be nationally representative. However, they said the trends it showed were convincing. Smaller studies also have found sharp declines in out-of-pocket spending, though experts said Tuesday's study was the largest to date.

"I find this study persuasive and consistent with what other studies are finding," said Alina Salganicoff, the director of women's health policy at the Kaiser Family Foundation, a health policy research group, who did not take part in the study. "I think we're seeing a clear pattern in the research."

The study did not address whether free or cheaper birth control led to fewer unintended pregnancies. Findings from pilot studies in St. Louis and Colorado suggested that when cost was not an issue, birth control use increased and women tended to choose the most effective methods, such as long-acting intrauterine devices and implants. That helped drive down rates of abortion and unintended pregnancy in both states.

"We have no doubt that the cost makes a difference," said Diana Zuckerman, the president of the National Center for Health Research in Washington. "When you have free contraception, it's going to affect pregnancy and abortion as well because money matters."

Contraception coverage has improved drastically since the early 1990s, with most insurance companies now covering the full range of birth control methods. But women still had to bear some cost, a requirement that experts say discouraged some lower-income women from getting it and that the Affordable Care Act largely eliminated.

"Co-payments were part of the movement to dissuade people from getting unnecessary care, but they ended up dissuading people from getting necessary care too," said Adam Sonfield, a senior policy analyst at the Guttmacher Institute, which tracks reproductive health measures and policies.

The study comes amid growing calls for birth control to be available to women over the counter, a change that some women's groups and professional medical societies support. Such a step would require approval from the Food and Drug Administration, and a Republican bill in the Senate would encourage companies to apply for over-the-counter status for their products.

Opponents have criticized the Republican legislation, saying it could reduce access for women if it meant that birth control was no longer covered in full. (Plans are required to cover most prescription medication, but not over-the-counter medication.) Senator Patty Murray, a Democrat from Washington who helped write the Affordable Care Act, called birth control "an extremely important part of women's health care and their costs."

Some Democrats in Congress note that many of the Republican sponsors of the bill on over-the-counter sales have voted to repeal the Affordable Care Act, which mandated the provision of free prescription contraceptives. Republicans say their bill does not take away women's right to get birth control with a prescription, it simply increases women's options.

The Affordable Care Act requires insurance plans to cover the full cost of preventive services, including prescription contraception. The mandate for contraception began in August 2012, and insurers were supposed to comply by the beginning of new plan periods, which for many women was Jan. 1, 2013.

Researchers used data from 2008 as a baseline for spending on prescription contraception, but their analysis compared spending in the first six months of 2012 with that in the first six months of 2013, when the mandate was in effect.

Average spending on the pill dropped by about half to $117 for the first six months of 2013, compared with $244 in the first six months of 2012. Spending per prescription — which can be up to three months of the pill — fell to $20.37 from $32.74. Spending on intrauterine devices declined by about 70 percent to about $110. (That includes the cost of insertion but not of removal.)

Average spending on implants, small devices inserted under the skin that prevent pregnancy for several years, declined by about 72 percent to about $91 per device. The steepest decline was for emergency contraception, which fell by more than 90 percent to an average of $1.75 per prescription.

Birth control represented about 44 percent of out-of-pocket spending on medical care in the first six months of 2012 among women in the study. That share had declined to about 22 percent in the first half of 2013. The age groups represented in the study tend to have relatively few health problems.

There were many reasons spending did not fall to zero, said Nora Becker, one of the study's authors. Health plans phased in the requirement, so the change did not happen immediately for everyone, and not all brands were required to be covered. Some older plans were grandfathered — about a third of all plans in 2013, according to the study — and others received an exemption for religious reasons. Some plans continued to leave some costs uncovered, a pattern that the Obama administration has warned against.

Spending on two methods in the data remained largely unchanged — the ring and the patch — a pattern some experts attributed to that sporadic coverage.

Courts Support Obama's Contraceptive Policy, but Challenges Remain

BY ROBERT PEAR | JULY 12, 2015

WASHINGTON — Four federal appeals courts have upheld efforts by the Obama administration to guarantee access to free birth control for women, suggesting that the government may have found a way to circumvent religious organizations that refuse to provide coverage for some or all forms of contraception.

While pleased with the rulings, administration officials are not celebrating.

Another federal appeals court, based in Denver, is considering a challenge to the same federal policy by the Little Sisters of the Poor, an order of Roman Catholic nuns who operate homes for low-income older people. At a hearing in December, a three-judge panel asked tough questions of lawyers on both sides of that case.

Moreover, lawyers say, even if the birth control policy is ultimately upheld in court, the government could face practical problems lining up third parties to pay for contraceptives over an employer's objections.

Sister Constance Veit, a spokeswoman for the Little Sisters of the Poor, said: "We live our lives very far from the public eye. We are not political activists at all. But we fear that the mandate could set a precedent for greater government intrusion into our ministry.

"Our health plans have never included contraceptives, and we've never had any complaints," Sister Constance said. "It has never been an issue for our staff."

The appeals court decisions, in favor of the government, involve a wide range of nonprofit religious organizations that are eligible for a dispensation from rules requiring employers to cover birth control for

GABRIELLA DEMCZUK FOR THE NEW YORK TIMES

Sister Joseph Mary assisted Eva Howse, 91, at the Jeanne Jugan Residence in Washington. The home is run by the Little Sisters of the Poor, who oppose a federal birth control rule.

women. On Friday, the administration offered similar relief to certain closely held for-profit corporations that oppose covering contraceptives because of the owners' religious beliefs.

Some nonprofit religious groups are still battling the administration in court, and some for-profit employers might do so, but the appeals court decisions will bolster the government's position.

In a typical opinion, Judge Richard A. Posner of the United States Court of Appeals for the Seventh Circuit, in Chicago, wrote this month, "When Wheaton College tells us that it is being 'forced' to allow 'use' of its health plans to cover emergency contraceptives, it is wrong."

In fact, Judge Posner wrote, the college — a Christian school in Illinois — is required only to inform its insurers or the government "that it will not use its health plans to cover emergency contraception, that it is out of the loop."

Under the Affordable Care Act, employers with 50 or more full-time employees are generally required to offer health coverage or pay substantial penalties. Under federal rules, the insurance must cover preventive services, including all forms of contraception approved for women by the Food and Drug Administration.

Houses of worship, including churches, temples and mosques, are automatically exempt from the contraceptive coverage requirement and do not have to file any paperwork.

Another group of employers — nonprofit religious organizations that object to such coverage on religious grounds — are eligible for an "accommodation": They are deemed to comply with the requirement if they report their objections to their health insurance companies and the administrators of their health plans, or to the secretary of health and human services.

This arrangement, which some judges call an opt-out mechanism, is available to certain schools and universities, hospitals and charities.

Many Roman Catholic, Baptist and other religious groups have challenged the opt-out procedure, saying it makes them complicit in providing contraceptive coverage. But so far they have lost in federal appeals courts in the District of Columbia, Philadelphia, Chicago and New Orleans.

"The plaintiffs have not shown a substantial burden on their religious exercise," Judge Jerry E. Smith wrote last month in an opinion for a three-judge panel of the United States Court of Appeals for the Fifth Circuit, in New Orleans.

Plaintiffs in that case, led by East Texas Baptist University, argued that the opt-out procedure violated a federal law, the Religious Freedom Restoration Act of 1993, because it forced them to "facilitate" the coverage of contraceptives.

When an employer objects to providing contraceptive coverage for religious reasons, the insurer or administrator of its group health plan is supposed to pay for the contraceptives, at no cost to women or the employer. The insurer must make clear to women that their employer

GABRIELLA DEMCZUK FOR THE NEW YORK TIMES

Sister Celestine offered communion in the home's chapel. The contraception policy is an attempt to address religious organizations that refuse to provide coverage.

does not provide or pay for contraceptive benefits. The federal government has several ways to reimburse insurers.

After analyzing these requirements, the United States Court of Appeals for the District of Columbia Circuit rejected challenges by Priests for Life, Catholic University of America and other Roman Catholic groups.

"Religious nonprofits that opt out are excused from playing any role in the provision of contraceptive services, and they remain free to condemn contraception in the clearest terms," wrote Judge Cornelia T. L. Pillard of the appeals court here. The Affordable Care Act, she wrote, "imposes an independent obligation" on insurers and third-party administrators to provide coverage.

Adam C. Jed, a Justice Department lawyer, explained that when a nonprofit religious group refuses to provide contraceptive coverage, "the government then steps in and fills the gap."

But that arrangement is abhorrent to some religious groups like the Little Sisters of the Poor, because the government can rely on information provided by the employer.

"The action of the religious employer is the trigger for contraceptive coverage," said Mark L. Rienzi, a lawyer at the Becket Fund for Religious Liberty, who represents the nuns. "The government wants to use our plan and our plan's information to provide this coverage."

Some judges disagree.

"Far from 'triggering' the provision of contraceptive coverage," the opt-out is a way for employers to declare that they "will not be complicit" in providing such coverage, wrote Judge Marjorie O. Rendell of the United States Court of Appeals for the Third Circuit, in Philadelphia.

Critics of the contraceptive coverage requirement won a major victory when the Supreme Court ruled last year in favor of Hobby Lobby Stores and two other closely held family-owned corporations that objected to certain forms of birth control. Forcing those companies to provide contraceptive coverage to their employees violates the 1993 law protecting religious freedom, the court said.

Justices Samuel A. Alito Jr. and Anthony M. Kennedy praised the opt-out procedure for nonprofit groups as an alternative to the all-or-nothing mandate imposed on companies like Hobby Lobby.

The opt-out "achieves all of the government's aims while providing greater respect for religious liberty," Justice Alito wrote.

Federal appeals courts have cited those comments as a reason to uphold the administration's latest effort to guarantee access to contraceptive coverage for women insured by Roman Catholic hospitals, universities and charities.

Better Contraception for Young Women

EDITORIAL | BY THE NEW YORK TIMES | JULY 13, 2015

COLORADO HAS ACHIEVED remarkable reductions in the rate of teenage pregnancy in recent years by giving young women free, long-acting contraceptives that protect them for several years. The birthrate among teenagers in the state plummeted by 40 percent from 2009 to 2013 and teenage abortions dropped by 42 percent largely as a result of this initiative.

Credit the Colorado Department of Public Health and Environment for an aggressive outreach program and wise use of private money to carry out a program that could not win approval from the state's legislature, the General Assembly. The department used funds from a private foundation to provide women with long-acting contraceptives at little or no cost. More than 30,000 intrauterine devices (IUDs) and contraceptive implants were distributed at 68 family planning clinics across the state.

The contraceptive implant is a small plastic rod, about the size of a matchstick, that contains a small amount of hormones and is inserted just under the skin of the upper arm. It can prevent pregnancy for three years once inserted and can be easily removed at any time; fertility immediately returns to normal. The IUDs provided are effective for at least five years, according to the department.

The department also used the private money to train their staff members on how long-acting contraceptives work and how to counsel women on their use.

These contraceptives have big advantages over the birth control pills, spermicides and condoms that poor women typically rely on, though condoms play an important role in preventing sexually transmitted disease. The failure rate of the implants and IUDs is minuscule, which reduces unplanned pregnancies and in turn makes it easier for young women to finish high school or college and enter the work force.

Greater use of these contraceptives can save taxpayers money by reducing spending on prenatal care, deliveries and post-pregnancy care for poor mothers and their children. The state health department estimates that every dollar spent on the long-lasting contraceptive program saved $5.85 for the state Medicaid program, which covers more than three-quarters of teenage pregnancies and births.

Unfortunately, the private grant is running out and the department has been searching, so far unsuccessfully, for additional funds to keep the effort going. As a smart budgetary move, the state General Assembly ought to provide the needed funds.

While birthrates and abortion rates among teenagers have dropped in the nation as a whole, researchers at the Colorado health department believe its efforts and the timing and magnitude of the reductions in their state constitute "a radical game change."

The Affordable Care Act requires insurance plans to cover contraceptives and related services, such as inserting and removing devices, at no cost to women. But various loopholes have left some women exposed to cost-sharing charges. Federal and state regulators and legislators need to close the remaining gaps as quickly as possible to ensure that every woman has easy access to the kinds of contraceptives that have produced such remarkable results in Colorado.

The New Era of Abstinence

EDITORIAL | BY THE NEW YORK TIMES | MAY 5, 2018

THE ADMINISTRATION OF Donald Trump — who had a child out of wedlock after cheating on his first wife, and is in a legal battle with a porn star who says she had sex with him not long after his third wife gave birth — is promoting abstinence with a zeal perhaps never before seen from the federal government.

Mr. Trump's Department of Health and Human Services is quietly advancing an anti-science, ideological agenda. The department last year prematurely ended grants to some teen pregnancy prevention programs, claiming weak evidence of success. More recently, it set new funding rules that favor an abstinence-only approach. In reality, programs that use creative ways to educate teenagers about contraception are one reason teen pregnancy in the United States has plummeted in recent years.

The administration is promoting a "just say no" approach to adults as well as to teenagers. It's poised to shift Title X family planning dollars — funds largely intended to help poor adult women around the United States get birth control — toward programs that advocate abstinence outside of marriage, as well as unreliable forms of birth control like the rhythm method (though the health agency might have to reverse course if either of the lawsuits filed against it last week by Planned Parenthood and other women's health advocates are successful).

Nor are its sights limited to the United States. As BuzzFeed News reported, administration officials who attended recent closed-door meetings at the United Nations were preoccupied with abstinence. Bethany Kozma, a senior adviser for gender equality and women's empowerment at the United States Agency for International Development, called America a "pro-life nation," stunning delegates from other countries.

CHLOE SCHEFFE

The administration's approach defies all common sense. There is no good evidence that abstinence-only education prevents or delays young people from having sex, leads them to have fewer sexual partners or reduces rates of teen pregnancy or sexually transmitted infections. And given that almost all Americans engage in premarital sex, this vision of an abstinent-outside-of-marriage world is simply at odds with reality.

Abstinence-only education also spreads misinformation. A 2004 government report found that many such curriculums undersold the effectiveness of condoms and made unscientific assertions, like a claim that a 43-day-old fetus is a "thinking person." This kind of propaganda also promotes gender stereotypes. "Women gauge their happiness and judge their success by their relationships," one curriculum taught students. "Men's happiness and success hinge on their accomplishments."

Public health experts strongly recommend a comprehensive approach to sex education, one that informs young people about abstinence as well as about various forms of contraception and other aspects of sexual health.

The Trump administration has lurched rightward, not just compared to the Obama administration, which funded some abstinence-only programs, but even compared to the Bill Clinton and George W. Bush eras, when federal funding for abstinence was much more robust than under Barack Obama.

Meanwhile, officials pushing these changes — including Valerie Huber, who once ran a national organization dedicated to promoting abstinence and now leads the Title X program at the health agency — have engaged in a savvy rebranding campaign. They use innocuous sounding terms like "sexual risk avoidance" and "healthy relationships" because they know "abstinence" can sound harsh and retrograde.

Disinformation is at the center of this agenda. It makes it more difficult for women to acquire the knowledge they need to control if and when they become pregnant — a problem that is exacerbated by the administration's hostility toward abortion rights. Beyond that, abstinence-only education keeps all people who are subjected to it in the dark about critical aspects of their health, and treats a normal part of life — sexuality, and women's sexuality in particular — as aberrant and shameful.

Trump Administration to Revise Birth Control Exemptions in Hopes of Saving Them

BY ROBERT PEAR | OCT. 30, 2018

WASHINGTON — Having lost in two federal courts and fearing more setbacks, the Trump administration is revising rules that allow employers to deny women insurance coverage for contraceptives based on religious or moral objections.

Administration officials hope that the changes, the details of which remain unclear, will overcome the judges' objections without fundamentally altering the purpose or the effects of the rules.

White House officials have cleared the revised rules so they can be issued jointly by the secretary of health and human services, Alex M. Azar II; Labor Secretary Alexander Acosta; and Treasury Secretary Steven Mnuchin.

It is unclear whether the administration intends to issue the final rules before the midterm elections next week. Opinion polls suggest that the birth control benefit, mandated by the Obama administration under the Affordable Care Act, is popular.

On its website, the White House Office of Management and Budget says it has finished reviewing the new rules, which will have the force of law.

"These final rules expand exemptions to protect religious beliefs for certain entities and individuals whose health plans are subject to a mandate of contraceptive coverage," the website says. And it describes the rule protecting "moral convictions" in the same way.

Opponents of the original rules, issued last October, have vowed to continue their fight.

"Our resolve to protect a woman's access to essential health care, including birth control, has not and will not waver," Attorney General

Xavier Becerra of California, one of the states that sued to block the rules, said on Tuesday.

Richard B. Katskee, the general counsel of Americans United for Separation of Church and State, which is supporting California's challenge, said: "The rules put in place a year ago by the Trump administration were unlawful and unconstitutional. We fully expect the new rules to be just as illegal."

The Affordable Care Act generally requires employers and insurers to provide preventive health services at no charge. The Obama administration defined those services to include all methods of contraception approved for women by the Food and Drug Administration.

Under rules issued in 2017, the Trump administration expanded exemptions from the contraceptive coverage mandate, allowing employers to opt out if they had religious or moral objections. Judge Wendy Beetlestone of the Federal District Court in Philadelphia blocked the administration in December, saying the Affordable Care Act did not authorize such "sweeping exemptions."

Judge Haywood S. Gilliam Jr. of the Federal District Court in Oakland, Calif., blocked the rules a week later. For a substantial number of women, he said, the rules would "transform contraceptive coverage from a legal entitlement to an essentially gratuitous benefit wholly subject to their employer's discretion."

Under the 2017 rules, he said, "more employers than ever before are eligible for the exemption."

The Trump administration has appealed both decisions. And the new rules are unlikely to end the legal fight over contraceptive coverage, which has been raging in courts around the country for more than six years.

The Little Sisters of the Poor, an order of Roman Catholic nuns, told the United States Court of Appeals for the Ninth Circuit, in San Francisco, last week that it should rule on the critical legal questions in the case "even if and when the agencies issue yet another version of their rule."

Among those questions is whether the religious exemption is legal or whether it violates provisions of the Constitution barring the establishment of religion and guaranteeing equal protection of the laws.

Mr. Trump's efforts to roll back the contraceptive coverage mandate were inspired, in part, by the Little Sisters. "I will make absolutely certain religious orders like the Little Sisters of Poor are not bullied by the federal government because of their religious beliefs," he said a month before the 2016 election.

One challenge to the Trump administration rules was filed by the State of California, joined by Delaware, Maryland, New York and Virginia. The other was filed by Pennsylvania.

The states said they would suffer economic harm as a result of the rules because they would have to provide contraceptive coverage or pay for medical treatment and social services for more women with unintended pregnancies.

The administration rejected that argument, saying it was based on a "speculative chain of contingencies."

"A woman who loses coverage of her chosen contraceptive method through her employer may still have access to such coverage through a spouse's plan," the Justice Department said in a brief. "Or she may otherwise be able to pay out of pocket for contraceptive services."

The states have not identified any "particular woman who will lose coverage" as a result of the rules, the Justice Department said.

The Obama administration cited studies showing that as the use of contraceptives went up, the rate of unintended pregnancies came down. But the Trump administration said these studies did not prove a causal link.

Trump Proposes a New Way Around Birth Control Mandate: Religious Exemptions and Title X

BY ROBERT PEAR | NOV. 17, 2018

WASHINGTON — The Trump administration is making it easier for employers to exclude birth control from health insurance benefits provided under the Affordable Care Act, and it has come up with a new justification, saying that female employees can obtain contraceptives at family planning clinics for low-income people.

That, in turn, could increase demand for clinic services, which are already squeezed. The plan is one of several recent proposals that could affect access to birth control, such as requiring the physical separation of services at clinics and strict new rules about insurance payments.

The health law generally requires employers to cover preventive health services, and the government says those include contraceptives for women. Under final rules published this past week, employers can obtain an exemption if they object to some or all forms of contraception based on their "sincerely held religious beliefs" or moral convictions.

In a separate proposed rule, the Trump administration said that women denied contraceptive coverage by their employers would be eligible for the family planning program created by Congress in 1970 under Title X of the Public Health Service Act.

Clinics in that program serve four million people a year, primarily low-income women and adolescents. Clinics must give priority to members of low-income families, defined as those with annual incomes less than or equal to the poverty level ($20,780 for a family of three).

Demand for clinic services already exceeds what can be provided with the available funds, $286.5 million a year.

Under the Trump administration's proposal, some women would be eligible for free contraceptives regardless of their income.

The proposed rule says that "a woman can be considered from a 'low-income family' if she has health insurance coverage through an employer" that, for religious or moral reasons, refuses to cover the contraceptives she seeks.

Administration officials said the proposed rule, issued by Alex M. Azar II, the secretary of health and human services, would meet the needs of women while deflecting legal challenges to the president's birth control policy.

The proposed rule will "preserve conscience protections" for employers and provide free or low-cost family planning services for women who need them, the administration said.

But Clare Coleman, the president and chief executive of the National Family Planning and Reproductive Health Association, which represents many clinics, said the proposal would "hijack Title X programs and use their limited federal funds to subsidize employers' refusal to comply with the contraceptive coverage requirement."

Groups that have fought the contraceptive coverage mandate, like the Little Sisters of the Poor, an order of Roman Catholic nuns, praised the policy.

"It shows that the government has ways of delivering contraceptive services without conscripting the Little Sisters of the Poor to help," said Mark L. Rienzi, the president of the Becket Fund for Religious Liberty, which represents the nuns in several court cases.

Gregory S. Baylor, a lawyer at the Alliance Defending Freedom, a conservative Christian group, said: "With these regulations, President Trump kept his promise that people of faith would not be bullied on his watch. At the same time, contraceptives will remain readily available to those who wish to use them."

The latest moves by the administration will face close scrutiny after Democrats take control of the House in January.

Representative Nita M. Lowey of New York, the senior Democrat on the House Appropriations Committee, has tried to block the new family planning rule. Her efforts were stymied by Republicans this year, but Ms. Lowey is in line to become the chairwoman of the committee next year, giving her more leverage over the administration.

Federal law, unchanged since 1970, says that Title X funds cannot be used in "programs where abortion is a method of family planning." The current rules, adopted by the Clinton administration in 2000, say that clinics must give pregnant women an opportunity to receive information and counseling on prenatal care, infant care, adoption and "pregnancy termination."

The Trump administration has proposed sweeping changes to those rules to "ensure that federal funds are not used to fund the abortion industry in violation of the law."

Representative Diana DeGette, Democrat of Colorado, has criticized the move, saying "the Trump administration is working furiously to turn back the clock on women's rights."

President Trump has also proposed eliminating the requirement for clinics to provide abortion-related information, counseling and referrals on request. As a result, the administration said, Title X funds would be available to "health care providers who refuse to participate in abortion-related activity such as counseling and referrals."

Under the current rules, clinics that receive Title X funds must provide a broad range of "medically approved family planning methods." The Trump administration's proposal would delete the words "medically approved." The proposal also makes clear that clinics would not have to provide every effective method of contraception.

In contrast, insurers and employer-sponsored health plans are generally required to cover all forms of contraception that have been approved for women by the Food and Drug Administration.

The Trump administration is also proposing stringent rules to require the physical separation of family planning and abortion services at clinics that offer both. Federal health officials estimate that 10 percent to 20 percent of Title X sites do not comply and would have to spend an average of $20,000 each to meet the proposed requirement.

Mr. Trump would like to go even further. His goal, he told an anti-abortion group in May, was to "prohibit Title X funding from going to any clinic that performs abortions."

Under the Affordable Care Act, insurers are allowed to cover abortions but cannot use federal money to help pay for the coverage. Insurers are allowed to send consumers a single monthly bill itemizing the amount of the premium earmarked for abortion and for other coverage, and consumers can pay the entire premium with one check.

The Trump administration proposed this month to tighten requirements for separate billing and payment. Insurers would have to send the bills in separate envelopes with separate postage, or in separate emails, and consumers would be instructed to make separate payments by check or electronic funds transfer.

Glossary

abortifacient A drug that terminates a pregnancy.

abortion The act of terminating a pregnancy.

abstinence Restraining from participating in something, such as drinking alcohol or sex.

cervix The lower part of the uterus; a passage through which a baby travels when being born.

combination pill A type of birth control pill that contains both estrogen and progesterone and prevents an egg from being released during ovulation.

Comstock Act A set of federal laws passed by Congress in 1873 that restricted using the U.S. Postal Service to send "obscene" information, including pornography and information about birth control or abortifacients. In response to the passage of the Comstock Act, many states passed their own Comstock laws.

conception The act of conceiving a child.

contraception The deliberate use of drugs, devices, or techniques to prevent pregnancy during sexual intercourse.

diaphragm A thin cap that fits over the cervix and prevents sperm from passing through to fertilize the egg; a birth control device.

estrogen Steroid hormones that are released in women's bodies to maintain their sexual and reproductive functions.

eugenics The science of controlling population growth by limiting reproduction, especially to decrease reproduction amongst people with so-called "undesirable" traits. Eugenics was incredibly popular as a science until the Nazis used and perverted the doctrines of eugenics during World War II.

fertilization The process by which male sperm fuses with a female egg to create a zygote, which will develop into a baby.

gynecologist A doctor that specializes in dealing with the functions and diseases of women's reproductive organs.

implantation The moment when a fertilized egg implants into a woman's uterus; this is a necessary step in conception.

intrauterine device (IUD) A metal device that is implanted in a woman's uterus to prevent a fertilized egg from implanting; a contraceptive device.

morning-after pill An emergency birth control pill that women can take up to seventy-two hours after unprotected sex to prevent pregnancy. Depending on the pill and the time during which it is taken, it can prevent ovulation or prevent fertilization or implantation.

ovulation The act of releasing an egg from the ovary; a woman must ovulate in order to get pregnant, and many birth control pills work by preventing ovulation.

progesterone A steroid that is released in women's bodies to prepare for pregnancy; progesterone is used in many birth control pills to block ovulation by tricking the body into believing it is already pregnant.

promiscuity Being characterized by having many sexual relationships.

rhythm method A natural birth control method in which sexual intercourse is avoided during the times during a women's menstrual cycle when she is likely to ovulate.

sterilization Surgery used to prevent a person or animal from being able to have children.

Media Literacy Terms

"Media literacy" refers to the ability to access, understand, critically assess and create media. The following terms are important components of media literacy, and they will help you critically engage with the articles in this title.

angle The aspect of a news story that a journalist focuses on and develops.

balance Principle of journalism that both perspectives of an argument should be presented in a fair way.

credibility The quality of being trustworthy and believable, said of a journalistic source.

critical review A type of story that describes an event or work of art, such as a theater performance, film, concert, book, restaurant, radio or television program, exhibition or musical piece, and offers critical assessment of its quality and reception.

editorial Article of opinion or interpretation.

feature story Article designed to entertain as well as to inform.

human interest story A type of story that focuses on individuals and how events or issues affect their life, generally offering a sense of relatability to the reader.

impartiality Principle of journalism that a story should not reflect a journalist's bias and should contain balance.

intention The motive or reason behind something, such as the publication of a news story.

interview story A type of story in which the facts are gathered primarily by interviewing another person or persons.

inverted pyramid A method of writing a story using facts in order of importance, beginning with a lead and then gradually adding paragraphs in order of relevance from most interesting to least interesting.

motive The reason behind something, such as the publication of a news story or a source's perspective on an issue.

news story An article or style of expository writing that reports news, generally in a straightforward fashion and without editorial comment.

op-ed An opinion piece that reflects a prominent individual's opinion on a topic of interest.

paraphrase The summary of an individual's words, with attribution, rather than a direct quotation of their exact words.

quotation The use of an individual's exact words indicated by the use of quotation marks and proper attribution.

reliability The quality of being dependable and accurate, said of a journalistic source.

rhetorical device Technique in writing intending to persuade the reader or communicate a message from a certain perspective.

source The origin of the information reported in journalism.

style A distinctive use of language in writing or speech; also a news or publishing organization's rules for consistent use of language with regards to spelling, punctuation, typography and capitalization, usually regimented by a house style guide.

tone A manner of expression in writing or speech.

Media Literacy Questions

1. Identify the various sources cited in the article "The Pill: Revolution in Birth Control" (on page 99). How does Jane E. Brody attribute information to each of these sources in her article? How effective are her attributions in helping the reader identify her sources?

2. In "Poverty and the Pill" (on page 177), Nicholas Kristof paraphrases information from interviews he has conducted. What are the strengths of using a paraphrase as opposed to a direct quote? What are the weaknesses?

3. Compare the headlines of "Poll Finds Shift in Views on Pill" (on page 109) and "To Them, Two Children Are Fine, But Three Crowd the World" (on page 111). Which is a more compelling headline, and why? How could the less compelling headline be changed to better draw the reader's interest?

4. What type of article is "Moralists at the Pharmacy" (on page 168)? Can you identify another article in this collection that is the same type of article?

5. Does Jane E. Brody demonstrate the journalistic principle of balance in her article "Why a Lag in Male-Oriented Birth Control?" (on page 136)? If so, how did she do so? If not, what could she have included to make her article more balanced?

6. The article "What Every Girl Should Know" (on page 174) is an example of an op-ed. Identify how Gail Collins's attitude and tone help convey her opinion on the topic.

7. Does "Cash-for-Sterilization Plan Draws Addicts and Critics" (on page 145) use multiple sources? What are the strengths of using multiple sources in a journalistic piece? What are the weaknesses of relying heavily on only one or a few sources?

8. "Courts Support Obama's Contraceptive Policy, but Challenges Remain" (on page 193) features photographs. What do these photographs add to the article?

9. What is the intention of the article "The New Era of Abstinence" (on page 200)? How effectively does it achieve its intended purpose?

10. Analyze the authors' reporting in "Women for Birth Control" (on page 29) and "Control of Population" (on page 48). Do you think one journalist is more impartial in their reporting than the other? If so, why do you think so?

11. Often, as a news story develops, a journalist's attitude toward the subject may change. Compare "Insurers Flout Rule Covering Birth Control, Studies Find" (on page 186) and "Courts Support Obama's Contraceptive Policy, but Challenges Remain" (on page 193), both by Robert Pear. Did new information discovered between the publication of these two articles change Pear's perspective?

12. Identify each of the sources in "Poverty and the Pill" (on page 177) as a primary source or a secondary source. Evaluate the reliability and credibility of each source. How does your evaluation of each source change your perspective on this article?

Citations

All citations in this list are formatted according to the Modern Language Association's (MLA) style guide.

BOOK CITATION

THE NEW YORK TIMES EDITORIAL STAFF. *Birth Control.* New York: New York Times Educational Publishing, 2020.

ONLINE ARTICLE CITATIONS

ASBURY, EDITH EVANS. "Birth Control Issue Again Stirs Debate." *The New York Times*, 24 Aug. 1958, https://timesmachine.nytimes.com/timesmachine/1958/08/24/81864849.pdf.

BELLUCK, PAM. "Cash-for-Sterilization Plan Draws Addicts and Critics." *The New York Times*, 24 July 1999, https://www.nytimes.com/1999/07/24/us/cash-for-sterilization-plan-draws-addicts-and-critics.html.

BERGER, LESLIE. "After Long Hiatus, New Contraceptives Emerge." *The New York Times*, 10 Dec. 2002, https://www.nytimes.com/2002/12/10/health/after-long-hiatus-new-contraceptives-emerge.html.

BERGER, LESLIE. "Quest for Male 'Pill' Is Gaining Momentum." *The New York Times*, 10 Dec. 2002, https://www.nytimes.com/2002/12/10/health/quest-for-male-pill-is-gaining-momentum.html.

BINDER, DAVID. "Mother Sees Gain in Sterilization." *The New York Times*, 13 Sept. 1962, https://timesmachine.nytimes.com/timesmachine/1962/09/13/90590037.pdf.

BLANCHARD, KELLY. "Let the Pill Go Free." *The New York Times*, 22 June 2010, https://www.nytimes.com/2010/06/22/opinion/22blanchard.html.

BOFFEY, PHILIP M. "Injected Contraceptive: Hazard or Boon?" *The New York Times*, 11 Jan. 1983, https://www.nytimes.com/1983/01/11/science/injected-contraceptive-hazard-or-boon.html.

BRODY, JANE E. "A New Birth Pill Cuts Side Effects." *The New York Times*,

20 Jan. 1966, https://timesmachine.nytimes.com/timesmachine/1966/01/20/79283563.html.

BRODY, JANE E. "The Pill: Revolution in Birth Control." *The New York Times*, 31 May 1983, https://timesmachine.nytimes.com/timesmachine/1966/05/31/121722597.pdf.

BRODY, JANE E. "Pill Use Rivaled by Sterilization, Survey Indicates." *The New York Times*, 22 July 1977, https://www.nytimes.com/1977/07/22/archives/pill-use-rivaled-by-sterilization-survey-indicates.html.

BRODY, JANE E. "Why a Lag in Male-Oriented Birth Control?" *The New York Times*, 16 Oct. 1983, https://www.nytimes.com/1983/10/16/weekinreview/why-a-lag-in-male-oriented-birth-control.html.

COLLINS, GAIL. "What Every Girl Should Know." *The New York Times*, 8 May 2010, https://www.nytimes.com/2010/05/08/opinion/08collins.html.

DENNETT, MARY WARE. "Birth Control's Hunt for Sponsor." *The New York Times*, 26 Feb. 1926, https://timesmachine.nytimes.com/timesmachine/1922/02/26/103582190.html.

FUENTES, ANNETTE. "Beyond Birth Control: The Pill Tackles New Duties." *The New York Times*, 7 May 2002, https://www.nytimes.com/2002/05/07/health/beyond-birth-control-the-pill-tackles-new-duties.html.

HARRIS, GARDINER. "Morning-After-Pill Ruling Defies Norm." *The New York Times*, 8 May 2004, https://www.nytimes.com/2004/05/08/us/morning-after-pill-ruling-defies-norm.html.

KLEMESRUD, JUDY. "Planned Parenthood's New Head Takes a Fighting Stand." *The New York Times*, 3 Feb. 1978, https://www.nytimes.com/1978/02/03/archives/planned-parenthoods-new-head-takes-a-fighting-stand-watchdog.html.

KLEMESRUD, JUDY. "To Them, Two Children Are Fine, But Three Crowd the World." *The New York Times*, 12 Jan. 1971, https://www.nytimes.com/1971/01/12/archives/to-them-two-children-are-fine-but-three-crowd-the-world.html.

KRISTOF, NICHOLAS. "Poverty and the Pill." *The New York Times*, 20 May 2010, https://www.nytimes.com/2010/05/20/opinion/20kristof.html.

L., W. L. "New Anti-Fertility Compound." *The New York Times*, 13 Apr. 1958, https://timesmachine.nytimes.com/timesmachine/1958/04/13/89076737.pdf.

LAURENCE, WILLIAM L. "Birth Control Is Accepted by American Medical Body." *The New York Times*, 9 June 1937, https://timesmachine.nytimes.com/timesmachine/1937/06/09/94385364.pdf.

LYONS, RICHARD D. "Panic and Pregnancies Linked to Senate Inquiry on Birth

Pill." *The New York Times*, 25 Feb. 1970, https://timesmachine.nytimes.com/timesmachine/1970/02/25/76708325.html.

MALLON, WINIFRED. "Freer Data Urged on Birth Control." *The New York Times*, 13 Apr. 1938, https://timesmachine.nytimes.com/timesmachine/1938/04/13/96813961.pdf.

MAY, ELAINE TYLER. "Promises the Pill Could Never Keep." *The New York Times*, 24 Apr. 2010, https://www.nytimes.com/2010/04/25/opinion/25may.html.

THE NEW YORK TIMES. "Better Contraception for Young Women." *The New York Times*, 13 July 2015, https://www.nytimes.com/2015/07/13/opinion/better-contraception-for-young-.

THE NEW YORK TIMES. "Birth Control Ban Fought by Doctors." *The New York Times*, 14 Feb. 1931, https://timesmachine.nytimes.com/timesmachine/1931/02/14/98320119.html.

THE NEW YORK TIMES. "Birth Control Gets Court Indorsement." *The New York Times*, 13 Oct. 1916, https://timesmachine.nytimes.com/timesmachine/1916/10/13/104693022.html.

THE NEW YORK TIMES. "Birth Control Peril to Race." *The New York Times*, 23 Aug. 1932, https://timesmachine.nytimes.com/timesmachine/1932/08/23/100797792.pdf.

THE NEW YORK TIMES. "Birth Controllers Up Early for Trial." *The New York Times*, 5 Jan. 1917, https://timesmachine.nytimes.com/timesmachine/1917/01/05/118128564.html.

THE NEW YORK TIMES. "Birth Spacing Seen as Post-War Need." *The New York Times*, 22 Jan. 1947, https://timesmachine.nytimes.com/timesmachine/1947/01/22/88740261.pdf.

THE NEW YORK TIMES. "Control of Population." *The New York Times*, 15 May 1925, https://timesmachine.nytimes.com/timesmachine/1925/05/15/101665577.html.

THE NEW YORK TIMES. "Doctors Divided on Birth Control." *The New York Times*, 19 Nov. 1916, https://timesmachine.nytimes.com/timesmachine/1916/11/19/104694697.html.

THE NEW YORK TIMES. "Fight Is Renewed on Birth Control." *The New York Times*, 10 June 1930, https://timesmachine.nytimes.com/timesmachine/1930/06/10/96150306.pdf.

THE NEW YORK TIMES. "Finds Birth Control Wrecking Home Life." *The New York Times*, 10 June 1930, https://timesmachine.nytimes.com/timesmachine/1930/06/10/96150306.html.

THE NEW YORK TIMES. "First Birth Control Clinic to Open Here." *The New York*

Times, 13 Nov. 1921, https://timesmachine.nytimes.com/timesmachine/1921/11/13/113322658.html.

THE NEW YORK TIMES. "For State Inquiry Into Birth Control." *The New York Times*, 1 Feb. 1917, https://timesmachine.nytimes.com/timesmachine/1917/02/01/118131716.html.

THE NEW YORK TIMES. "Moralists at the Pharmacy." *The New York Times*, 3 Apr. 2005, https://www.nytimes.com/2005/04/03/opinion/moralists-at-the-pharmacy.html.

THE NEW YORK TIMES. "Mrs. Sanger Accepts Bail." *The New York Times*, 28 Oct. 1916, https://timesmachine.nytimes.com/timesmachine/1916/10/28/100225380.html.

THE NEW YORK TIMES. "The New Era of Abstinence." *The New York Times*, 5 May 2018, https://www.nytimes.com/2018/05/05/opinion/sunday/the-new-era-of-abstinence.html.

THE NEW YORK TIMES. "The Perfect Contraceptive: When?" *The New York Times*, 1 June 1985, https://www.nytimes.com/1985/07/01/opinion/the-perfect-contraceptive-when.html.

THE NEW YORK TIMES. "Poll Finds Shift in Views on Pill." *The New York Times*, 1 Mar. 1970, https://www.nytimes.com/1970/03/01/archives/poll-finds-shift-in-views-on-pill-more-women-see-a-danger-in-oral.html.

THE NEW YORK TIMES. "Progress on Birth Control Pill." *The New York Times*, 12 July 1959, https://timesmachine.nytimes.com/timesmachine/1959/07/12/89223191.pdf.

THE NEW YORK TIMES. "Talks of Birth Control." *The New York Times*, 20 Apr. 1915, https://timesmachine.nytimes.com/timesmachine/1916/04/20/105461977.html.

THE NEW YORK TIMES. "Want More Babies in Good Families." *The New York Times*, 25 Sept. 1921, https://timesmachine.nytimes.com/timesmachine/1921/09/25/98744440.html.

THE NEW YORK TIMES. "Women for Birth Control." *The New York Times*, 15 Oct. 1920, https://timesmachine.nytimes.com/timesmachine/1920/10/15/109333535.html.

THE NEW YORK TIMES. "Would Limit Families." *The New York Times*, 29 June 1915, https://timesmachine.nytimes.com/timesmachine/1915/06/29/104648906.html.

PEAR, ROBERT. "Courts Support Obama's Contraceptive Policy, but Challenges Remain." *The New York Times*, 13 July 2015, https://www.nytimes.com/2015/07/13/us/politics/courts-support-obamas-contraceptive-policy-but-challenges-remain.html.

PEAR, ROBERT. "Insurers Flout Rule Covering Birth Control, Studies Find." *The New York Times*, 20 Apr. 2015, https://www.nytimes.com/2015/04/30/us/insurers-flout-rule-covering-birth-control-studies-find.html.

PEAR, ROBERT. "Trump Administration to Revise Birth Control Exemptions in Hopes of Saving Them." *The New York Times*, 30 Oct. 2018, https://www.nytimes.com/2018/10/30/us/politics/trump-birth-control-religious-exemptions.html.

PEAR, ROBERT. "Trump Proposes a New Way Around Birth Control Mandate: Religious Exemptions and Title X." *The New York Times*, 17 Nov. 2018, https://www.nytimes.com/2018/11/17/us/politics/trump-birth-control.html.

PECK, ELLEN. "Obituary: Motherhood." *The New York Times*, 13 May 1972, https://www.nytimes.com/1972/05/13/archives/obituary-motherhood.html.

PERLEZ, JANE. "Contraceptives' Presence in Schools Creates a Dispute Among Educators." *The New York Times*, 13 Oct. 1986, https://www.nytimes.com/1986/10/13/nyregion/issue-debate-contraceptives-presence-schools-creates-dispute-among-educators.html.

RABIN, RONI CARYN. "Morning-After Pill Is Not a Cure-All." *The New York Times*, 8 Apr. 2013, https://well.blogs.nytimes.com/2013/04/08/morning-after-pill-is-not-a-cure-all.

SCHMECK, HAROLD M., JR. "Birth Control Taboos Are Easing." *The New York Times*, 18 Nov. 1962, https://timesmachine.nytimes.com/timesmachine/1962/11/18/118441798.pdf.

SCHMECK, HAROLD M., JR. "Birth Pills Termed Still Experimental." *The New York Times*, 16 Jan. 1970, https://www.nytimes.com/1970/01/16/archives/birth-pills-termed-still-experimental-birth-pills-termed-still.html.

SCHWARTZ, HARRY. "The Fear That Birth Control May Mean 'Genocide.' " *The New York Times*, 2 May 1971, https://www.nytimes.com/1971/05/02/archives/the-fear-that-birth-control-may-mean-genocide-population.html.

SLADE, MARGOT, AND WAYNE BIDDLE. "Courts Block Federal Rule on Contraceptives." *The New York Times*, 20 Feb. 1983, https://www.nytimes.com/1983/02/20/weekinreview/ideas-and-trends-courts-block-federal-rule-on-contraceptives.html.

STROM, STEPHANIE. "Catholic Group Is Told to Pay for Birth Control." *The New York Times*, 2 Mar. 2004, https://www.nytimes.com/2004/03/02/us/catholic-group-is-told-to-pay-for-birth-control.html.

TAVERNISE, SABRINA. "After Health Care Act, Sharp Drop in Spending on Birth Control." *The New York Times*, 7 July 2015, https://www.nytimes.com/2015/07/08/health/after-health-care-act-sharp-drop-in-spending-on-birth-control.html.

Index

This book is current up until the time of printing. For the most up-to-date reporting, visit www.nytimes.com.